"An engaging, informa
boosting your confiden
practi
Michel

"An excellent style guide... particularly loved the
chapter on myth-busting. Every woman needs to
read this."
Amelia Taylor, Tortue.uk

"The Fashion Bible! Covers all areas and more to
really elevate your wardrobe."
Tara Blamey, Model

"All the information you have been trying to find on
how to look and feel good."
Jessica Noble

"Having seen Angela in action at one of our styling
events, we know she knows her stuff! What a joy to
have her advice written down in a book. Finding the
right colours that work for you will transform not only
your wardrobe but also how you feel – in this book
Angela helps you do just that plus great tips on how
to re-style your clothes to give them a new fresh
look."
Bel and Linzi, Dandi Cornwall

LOOK GOOD & FEEL
Fantastic

Thanks

Thank you to everyone who has helped me create this book.

To Nina for her inspiration that you can do anything you put your mind to and overcome the most difficult of challenges.

To my family and friends for putting up with chaos and my crazy ideas whilst supporting me from the sidelines (especially after re-discovering running, completing London Paris and New York Marathons over three successive years). I love you all!

And especially to Alison – the bravest lady I know, the funniest and the most stylish in First Class!

Contents

ANGELA YORKE

Introduction

This book aims to help anyone who feels like they need a bit of a steer to get themselves looking and feeling their best.

Most people gain knowledge from parents, siblings or friends...which is great if they know what they are doing! Sometimes, we don't have those people in our lives to steer us, and sometimes, life takes its toll. We lose ourselves along the way and don't always like or recognise the person looking back in the mirror.

I want to share all the information, style tips and tricks gained through my life experiences, from modelling as a teenager to working in fashion retail and styling.

It's not about looking good in someone else's eyes (although you will, and they will compliment you). It's about looking good and feeling good for yourself so that when you look in the mirror, you have the confidence to go out and conquer the world!

ANGELA YORKE

Chapter 1

Who Are You?

"No need for everyone to look the same. The secret is to wear what suits you best!"

Chica Umino

Have you ever noticed how some people seem to have "it"? They walk into a room just like everyone else, except people notice – they turn heads, receive compliments and ooze an aura of self-confidence and *je ne sais quoi,* as the French would put it.

Do you want to know what their secret is? How do they do it so effortlessly? Then this book is for you!

It starts with looking at yourself – not just a glance in the mirror but a "proper" look and getting to know who you are. The real "you" – not the "you" that you may think you are up until now.

As women, we often have many hats to wear, be it cook, chef, childminder, professional, cleaner, teacher, personal shopper and many more. It's easy to forget who we really are as we fulfil so many roles, often focussing on other people, but if you really want to find "it", you need to stop and take a look at who you are now, not who you were or who you want to be. You will only ooze that aura of self-confidence once you work that out, and that's the secret to "it"!

Sounds easy, hey? Or maybe it sounds daunting? Either way, it's time to look at yourself to discover your style personality, which colours suit you and identify your body shape. These are the first steps – a bit like building a house. These are the foundations and the starting point to looking and feeling good.

You also need to look at the life you lead – not what you used to do in the past and not what you would like to do in the future – literally what kind of lifestyle you lead, the things you do now and the environment you live in.

Perhaps you live in a coastal location, countryside location, or a town or city. The clothes you wear should be suitable for the life that you lead. There is no point in having a wardrobe full of "black tie do" dresses if you haven't been to a "black tie do" in the last 20 years! You wouldn't wear a city suit to walk the local public footpath either, would you? See what I mean?

Lifestyles change over time. We may go from ambitious career girl to life partner, perhaps becoming a busy parent ourselves until our children leave the nest. As we age, a new chapter of life (and menopause) opens up. Some keep a professional career going through all these stages; others put their career on hold and work in a way that fits their family or other commitments outside of work.

At each stage, we want different things and live life differently, perhaps living in entirely different locations too, so you need to bear in mind that your clothing collection will evolve over time, not just to fit lifestyles but also to fit changes that naturally happen to our bodies too.

Once you know your body shape, you can become a magician! Dressing well is partly about optical illusions and how you can trick the eye into seeing things differently. In this book, we will look at how you can use magic tricks when dressing to hide the parts of your body that you don't like while highlighting the bits you love. We will also destroy a few style myths and legends along the way that you may have been told growing up.

You may have "had your colours done" previously and come away with a little book of colour swatches that you abide by and never deviate from, or maybe you have no idea what I'm talking about! You may not know what colours suit you but have a favourite colour that you like to wear and tend to stick to.

We will look at outfit building and thinking outside the box regarding your clothing, ooooo the mystery and intrigue! So that you get value for money from your clothing purchases and avoid overbuying.

And that brings me to wardrobes...most of us are guilty of having wardrobes or drawers bursting at the seams when we only wear 20% of the garments we own. Sorting out your wardrobe is therapeutic and helps you look at your clothes to see which pieces go together to form outfits. It will also help you to understand why that top you bought in the sale is still on a hanger with the ticket attached unworn since you bought it three years ago.

Together, we will go through the steps to declutter your wardrobe and work out which pieces to keep, which pieces to let go of, how to store them, and how to look after them. As the fashion icon Vivienne Westwood once said, "Buy less, choose well and make it last!"

Looking good and feeling fantastic is not just about your clothes; it's also about your physical aspects – how you feel, what you eat and where your head is. Diet, nutrition, skincare, exercise and mental health all form part of creating that aura of self-confidence. Think of it as a bigger picture that your actual clothing is a small part of – a bit like a clockface – you can only tell the time when you see the whole clock face – if you look at just the hands, could you still tell what time it is?

During this book, we will go on a journey together to help you gain clarity, digging deep to identify who you are. You are in the driving seat, with me as your sat-nav to guide you along the way, with a few stopovers to pause and reflect.

This book is your route map to finding "it" for yourself, which is our destination for this trip. However, the journey continues as "it" will change in the years ahead, so buckle up – some bits will be a bit bumpy along the way, but I promise you it will be worth it.

Chapter 2
Style Personalities

"You cannot choose your face,
but you can choose your dress."
Amit Kalantri

The first step to finding clothing that makes you feel good and gives you confidence when you wear it is to consider your style personality.

Do you gravitate towards certain fabrics, styles, or colours when you shop for clothes? Or do you avoid printed fabrics? Like Marmite, you may love or loathe embellishments such as sequins.

All these things build into a picture that defines your style personality. Subconsciously, your style personality underpins the fabrics you prefer and the style of clothing you like to wear, but how do you know what style personality you are?

It's important to note that your style personality may change over time depending on what is happening in your life. When we go through them, you may identify with a particular one or more. There are no hard and fast rules. The style personalities are just a guide to help you understand your style likes and dislikes. Knowing your style personality makes clothes shopping so much easier as you can target certain brands or styles of clothing knowing that they will work for you, saving you time, money and mistakes when buying items for your wardrobe.

There are generally five style personalities:

- Natural

- Classic

- Dramatic

- Feminine/Romantic

- Artistic

You may find that a particular style resonates with you from your past and that a different style personality may be more who you are now. Concentrating on who you are now is essential as this will help you later when you look at decluttering your wardrobe, understanding why you may have things in there with tags still attached that you have never worn and probably never will!

Natural

A natural style personality opts to wear natural fabrics like cotton or viscose. Comfort is key. You have a more casual, informal style without faffy details like ruffles. The look is usually well put together, including cotton, denim, linen, cashmere and silk. You often wear soft or minimal makeup to keep with your natural clothing style. Accessories are usually kept to neutral shades and made from soft/flexible materials.

Classic

A classic style personality is a person with a more traditional, sometimes conservative, approach to what you wear. You may choose fabrics similar to a natural style; however, your look is more tailored, elegant, and refined. You like the design lines of your clothes to follow your body shape, opting for medium-weight quality fabrics. The look isn't dull or "old maid" but may feature classic fabrics such as tweeds, soft tartans or houndstooth prints in neutral shades like black, camel, navy or grey. Smooth, small geometric prints or polka dots that draw the eye may be paired with classic accessories like leather handbags or tote bags with traditionally practical footwear like loafers. A classic style personality often wears makeup in soft shades with coordinated eye and lip colours and a preference for neutral accessories such as simple belts and tote bags.

Dramatic

A dramatic style personality likes to wear something slightly different that makes you stand out. Usually, a bit quirky in your style, deliberately opting to wear something that turns heads. You like elegant lines such as asymmetric hems and sculptured tailoring in your outfits. Often, you go for bold, bright colours or prints with abstracts and striking designs. A dramatic style personality is usually characterised by a confident person. You like your little luxuries, so wear satin, silk and crepe fabrics. Your personality will fully embrace metallics, trends and big, bold floral prints. Luxurious accessories are preferred, such as luxury brand handbags and makeup that often feature noticeable dramatic eye makeup and bold lip colours.

Feminine/Romantic

A feminine/romantic style personality embraces a look that is feminine but not too "girly" with a preference for subtle romantic looks featuring soft flowing fabrics in softer shades that drape or ruffle. Favourite fabrics include chiffon, lace, or silk, often in tiny floral prints. The design lines of clothes enhance body shapes and usually feature a 50s style such as sweetheart necklines or 40s style tea dresses as well as more glamourous looks from pencil skirts that define the waist too. Your style personality will opt for soft makeup shades and a more "naturally made up" look with the occasional bold lip.

Artistic

An artistic style personality is often found in people who work in the creative arts industry. You love the drama of an outfit and are drawn to all prints, materials and bright colours, seeing fashion as a form of art. Creative and exotic prints or "out there" styles will catch your eye. You are likely to replicate a look exactly as seen in a catwalk show or magazine page, having the inner confidence to carry off a "different to the norm" look out on the street in day-to-day life. Inner confidence means that sometimes your style personality will wear no makeup or the exact opposite and go for very noticeable, strong and bold makeup instead.

As you read through these style personalities, you may think of a celebrity who oozes a particular style. You may also notice that certain retailers or clothing brands produce clothing aimed at certain style personalities, too. All of this helps to build a picture that will help you when you shop for clothes in the future, as you will know which stores/brands are more likely to have the kind of thing you are looking for so that you don't waste your time shopping in the wrong places.

Your lifestyle will inevitably impact your style personality. You may have a different style personality in your work life than in your home life. There are no hard and fast rules – the style personalities are a guide that you can use to help identify who you are when it comes to the clothes that you choose and like to wear.

If you feel totally bamboozled about where you sit regarding style personalities, look at the pieces you already have in your wardrobe that you wear the most. This can help you determine where your style personality sits today and how you can work with that base to improve your style as the person you want to be.

Consulting a personal stylist can be a fantastic idea to help steer your style ship in the right direction. Some larger retailers offer this service free or as a pay-for-service that can be redeemed against a purchase. Investing your time in a personal styling session can introduce you to things you don't realise will work for you. When you shop with friends, you may find that they will tell you what you want to hear when you try on clothes...or they may be brutally honest friends and say, "Oh no...that is not a good look on you." I remember trying on clothes in a changing room with my young son in tow and asking if he liked them on me – the answer was always "Yes Mummy, I think you should buy it" – not because it looked good, it was just because he wanted to get out of the shop.

A personal stylist will gently introduce you to styles you may not have considered before. They will encourage you to try new shapes and colours in clothing, which is essential. Often many things look like nothing when they are hanging flat on a hanger; but take on a totally different lease of life when tried on as the design features in the garment sit in specific places on the body that you can't replicate a hanger.

Homework

Look at the clothes you enjoy wearing and those you wear most often to see where they sit regarding your style personality.

Consider which style personality (or more than one) applies to you and ask yourself if this is the style for the person you still want to be in your current lifestyle.

See if there is a celebrity whose fashion style you admire and would like to replicate.

Consider trying a personal styling session for a wardrobe refresh if you find all the style personality advice a bit bamboozling or feel stuck in a rut.

Chapter 3

Body Shapes

"People hide behind the masks, but eventually you see them for who they truly are."

Amaka Imani Nkosazana

One of the key foundations of "it" is knowing your body shape, so it's time to take a long look in the mirror. For this, I recommend stripping back to your underwear to really analyse your own shape. It may be difficult for most people to do this as there are going to be bits of your body that you dislike but don't worry, we all have bits that we don't like. I bet that if you asked Supermodels like Naomi Campbell or Kate Moss they would agree with this too.

Remember, nobody is perfect. Whilst you might wish you were taller; a taller person might wish they were shorter. We are often our biggest critics when we analyse ourselves.

I recommend using a double mirror set-up so that you can look at your body shape from the rear and side angles, too. If you don't have access to two full-length mirrors, stand in front of one full-length mirror and use a small hand-held mirror to look back at the parts of your body you don't usually see.

Some body shapes are easily identifiable, with others a little more tricky, so make sure you take a really good look and use this guide to work out which body shape is most like you so that you can start to understand which styles of clothing will best suit your shape and which styles to avoid.

The aim of the game is to even out your shape by wearing clothing that gives the impression that your hips and shoulders are of a similar width, which is why identifying your body shape will really help you.

You may have heard of the "Rule of Thirds", the idea is that when you look at yourself in a mirror, the area of your body from the neck to your ankles should be split into three sections. For the optimum image, your eye should be drawn to the point that breaks up your silhouette at either the one-third or the two-thirds point. For example, suppose you have long legs occupying two-thirds of your silhouette and a shorter body that makes up one-third. Short, boxy jackets will be a good look but longer jackets that split your silhouette into two equal parts will make you look frumpy.

Body Shape Identification Guide

Body Shape A – Triangle Body Shape

- Does the top half of your body have a slimmer build than your hips?

- Do you wear a trouser/skirt size larger than the size you would wear in a jacket or top?

If so, then you are body shape A, which is a triangle shape (like the shape of a capital A)

A Shape

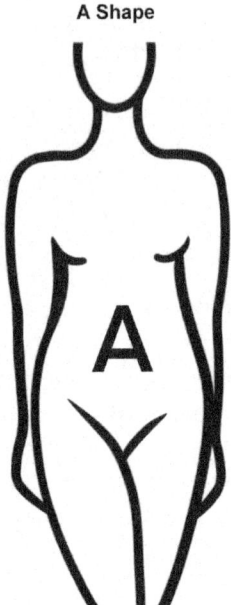

To look your best, choose dresses that show off your legs, diverting the eye away from the broadest part of your waist and hips.

Flared trousers or bootcut jeans will elongate the leg and flatter your silhouette, but avoid trousers that feature darts or side pockets, as these will make your hips look wider than they really are.

Choose jackets that fall below the hips to even out the width of your shoulders and hips, which will also help elongate your body.

Avoid wearing tops that stop at the widest point of your hips or accentuate the imbalance between your shoulders and hips.

Body Shape V – Inverted Triangle Body Shape

- When you look in the mirror, are your shoulders wider than your hips?

- Do you wear a trouser/skirt size smaller than the size you would wear in a jacket or top?

V Shape

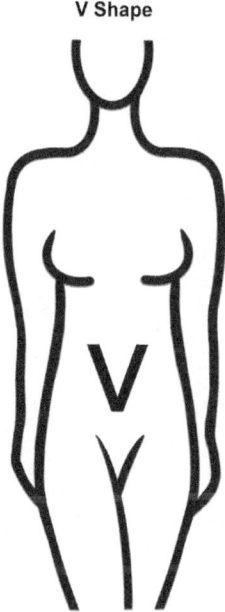

If so, then you are body shape V, which is an inverted triangle shape (like the shape of a capital V)

Opt for strapless, V-neck or asymmetrical necklines that add structure to your shoulder area to look your best. Round neck tops will soften your look as the eye is drawn down rather than across.

Straight cuts and A-line dresses and skirts look good on your body shape as they balance out your hips with your shoulders.

Avoid wearing thick "puffer" jackets, trench coats and jackets with wide collars, as these will accentuate the width of your shoulders even more. Also, avoid any tops or jackets with shoulder pads for the same reason.

Horizontal stripes and boat neck tops should be avoided as they accentuate your wider top half and make the eye think you are wider than you are.

Body Shape X – Hourglass Body Shape

- When you look in the mirror, are you in proportion?
- Are your shoulders the same width as your hips, and is your waist well-defined?

If so, you are body shape X, an hourglass body shape.

X Shape

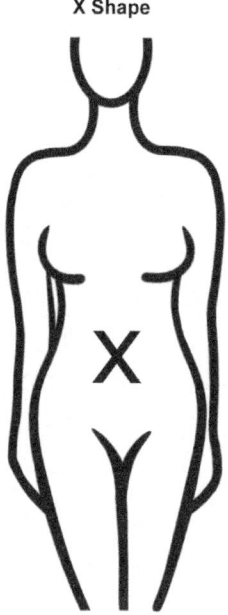

Even if you have a well-proportioned shape like this, there are still some things to avoid, to look your best.

Plunging necklines and V-neck tops suit your shape but avoid square necklines as they draw the eye to the wrong part of your body.

Fitted jackets and coats worn open will draw attention to the slimness of your waist, but avoid tops or jackets with well-defined shoulder pads, which will distort your proportions.

Pencil skirts, flared or straight skirts will also suit you.

Body Shape 8 – Figure of 8 Body Shape

- Are your shoulders the same width as your hips, and is your waist well-defined?

- Do you have full/large boobs?

If so, then you are body shape 8, which is a figure 8

8 Shape

body shape.

Fitted and low-cut tops in floaty fabrics will look fantastic on you, especially anything worn close to the body, like wrap tops.

Opt for high-waisted skirts and trousers and avoid loose, shapeless clothing that hides your shape, as this ruins your silhouette, making you look larger than you really are.

Body Shape H – Straight Body Shape

- Are your shoulders the same width as your hips?
- Are you small in size?
- Do you consider yourself to have an athletic build?

H Shape

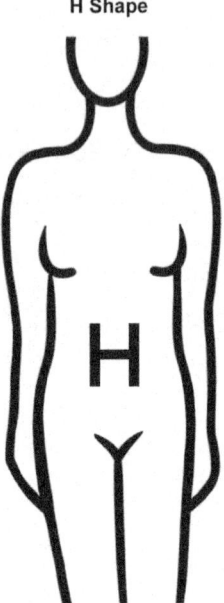

If so, you are body shape H, a straight or athletic build body shape.

Choose soft vests and feminine flowing blouses unless you want to rock a more masculine-tailored look.

Jackets that are lightly fitted and worn open, jumpers and anything with a high V neck will flatter you, along with empire line tunics and dresses that highlight your chest.

Avoid wearing anything that gives you more volume, like shoulder pads, turtlenecks or balloon sleeves on tops. Similarly, avoid horizontal striped tops and waist belts.

You need to avoid things that accentuate the rectangular shape of your silhouette, like a straight-cut skirt – opt for more voluminous skirts instead.

Body Shape O – Apple Body Shape

- Do you have rounded shoulders roughly the same width as your hips?

- Do you carry your weight around your middle?

- Do you have full/large boobs?

If so, you are body shape O (my personal favourite), an apple body shape that can initially be tricky to master.

O Shape

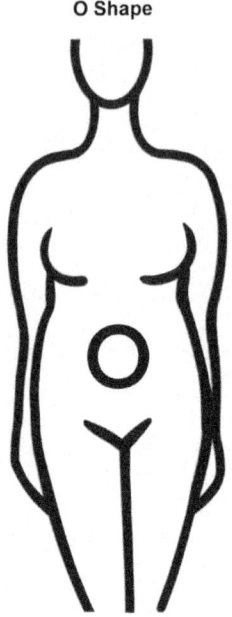

Avoid wearing clothes that are too big, as they will drown you and make you look larger than you are. However, if you opt for oversized clothing (a bit of a trend that comes and goes), try to disguise the areas where your weight sits and divert the attention away from your middle and up towards your neckline or down towards your feet.

Tops with shoulder pads and ¾ length sleeves that finish above the wrist (or push up your sleeves) will balance how the eye sees your silhouette.

Avoid tightly fitting detailing and choose a loose-fit top – but not too loose. Tops that feature a little slit in the sides of the hemline at the waist will work well for you as this helps to sit better across the top of your hips.

For the most flattering look, ensure that the top's hemline sits between your waist and finishes higher than the bottom of your bottom. This will hide your tummy and hips and finish at a more flattering length without making your legs look short.

Flat-fronted trousers work well for your shape, especially if they have wide legs and a side fastening, to keep details away from your middle. Equally, denim jeans in a darker colour with wide legs, flares or a classic boot cut will be most flattering.

Homework

Work out which body shape or shapes seem most like you, then note down as we revisit this later in the book.

Chapter 4

Colour Palettes

"Is the spring coming?...What is it like..."
Frances Hodgson Burnett

Now that you are starting to understand your style personality and body shape, it's time to think about colours and how to work out which colours are best for you.

The quick answer is to book a consultation with a colour expert (usually for a fee). Still, you may not have the cash, time or inclination to sit with a stranger for an hour with no makeup on whilst they hold lots of different coloured scarves up to your face in front of a mirror to show you what works and what doesn't.

The benefits of working with a colour expert are that they will help you work out the "iffy" colours – the ones that you are not quite sure about that you think might work but, on the other hand, may not be the right shade for you. You will also leave with a little wallet of colour swatches that suit you and are a handy guide when shopping.

There are alternatives if you don't want to go the professional colour consultation route. Some websites for clothes or makeup have short online tests where you are asked a series of questions. Depending on the answers you give, it generates colours of makeup or garments that might work for you. This will give you an idea of colours and tones that you can then use to assess which season of colour palette is your own.

Most people can wear any colour, provided they pick the right shade. For example, if fuschia pink doesn't suit you, choosing baby pink has the opposite effect and lifts your complexion so that when you look in a mirror, you like what you see and your eyes are all sparkly, too.

To find the colour palette that works for you, we need to look at your skin tone, eye colour and hair colour to ascertain whether warm tones or cooler tones are your thing. Some people swear by looking at the veins in their wrists. If they appear bluer, you will likely suit cooler colours. In contrast, you will likely suit warmer colours if they seem greener.

You may have been using 'trial and error' with colours, and I guarantee that there will be at least one colour in your wardrobe that you like to wear that makes you feel fantastic. This is a great starting point for finding more colours for outfits that bring you joy and confidence.

Colour palettes are based on the seasons, i.e. spring, summer, autumn, and winter and often reflect colours seen in nature during those seasons, too. Whatever season you identify as your own will stay with you for life and will not change as you age.

Spring colour palettes are warm colours like caramels and all the light, bright emerging colours of the season that you see in nature, such as bright blues, vibrant greens, yellows and tomato reds. Shades of ecru (or blossom shades) tend to work better than cool ice white.

People with a spring colour palette may have grey or blue eyes and a complexion that tans slightly.

Gold metallics will suit a spring colour palette more than silver, which is handy when we look at accessories later.

A spring colour palette can also borrow shades from an autumn colour palette as they work harmoniously together. A celebrity example of a spring colour palette is Kylie Minogue.

Autumn colour palettes are warm colours that often reflect the colours we see at this time of year when the leaves change. Think browns, greens, golds and rusty reds. Midnight blues work well rather than black as your darker shades.

People with an autumn palette may have red, auburn or dark brown hair, freckles and a sun-kissed complexion with green or brown coloured eyes. A celebrity example of an autumn colour palette is Julia Roberts.

An autumn colour palette can borrow shades from a spring colour palette with gold metallics most likely to suit you more than silver.

Summer colour palettes are cooler colours (a bit ironic, given that summer is supposed to be hot). Generally, these shades suit your typical English Rose complexion with pale skin and maybe blue eyes.

Just as the strength of the midday sun "whites out" colours, the shades that suit this colour palette are blues, pinks, creams and shades of off-white balanced with navy blue. Generally, paler colours feature along with pastels. However, a bright cobalt blue will suit, too – just like the colours of the sea in summer.

A celebrity example of a summer colour palette is Jennifer Aniston. This colour palette can also borrow shades from a winter colour palette. Silver will probably suit you more than gold when it comes to metallics.

Winter colour palettes are cooler and typically quite dark. Charcoal grey shades and black are great for this palette, especially when contrasted with bright jewel colours like fuschia pinks, vibrant purples and reds. Opt for ice whites rather than creamy shades of white.

You will likely be in the winter season if you have dark hair, dark brown eyes and an olive or richer skin tone. A celebrity example of a winter colour palette is Catherine Zeta-Jones.

When it comes to metallics, silver will most likely suit more than gold. You can also borrow shades from a summer colour palette.

You will notice that some colours appear in every season but are slightly different shades. Generally, red is a colour that suits everyone, provided you find the right shade and have the confidence to wear it. If you are new to experimenting with introducing colour to your wardrobe, you should build up to it gradually. There will be more about how to wear colours in a different chapter.

Whatever colours suit you, there are knock-on effects to consider in your makeup palette, too. If you are wearing pink colours in your clothing, you should generally wear pink shades in your makeup. Otherwise, the overall image isn't quite going to look right.

Similarly, if you wear shades of caramel and brown, your makeup should be bronze based, as the pink shades will clash and take away from your overall image.

Remember, changing your hair colour dramatically, going from blonde to brunette (or other colours) does not necessarily impact your colour analysis. Your natural shade is important, not the colour it may be right now. As many women change the colour of their hair, it's pretty rare to see people with their natural hair colour these days.

It's not just the items in your wardrobe that make you feel good; a decent haircut, and sometimes even a wash and blow dry, can make you feel like a new woman. If you change the colour of your hair regularly, you may want to consider whether that constant change in hair colour is such a good thing as, in all probability, the chemicals in the colour are probably not doing your hair any favours.

Homework

Look in the mirror to identify your skin tone, eye and hair colour.

Think about a colour that you already know suits you and identify if it is a warmer or cooler tone, then consider the descriptions of the seasons to see which one seems most like you.

If you struggle to work it out, remove your makeup and hold up different coloured garments or scarves next to your face. Look for the colours that brighten your complexion and avoid those that make you look washed out.

At the end of the day, if a colour makes you look and feel tired, this is not the best colour for you to wear in your clothing and may be better confined to accessories only.

ANGELA YORKE

Chapter 5

Magic Tricks; It's All An Illusion

"What a strange power there is in clothing."

Isaac Bashevis Singer

Having identified your body shape and an idea of the colours that suit you, it's time to look at your proportions to understand what you can do to hide those bits that you feel are your problem areas and enhance your best bits.

We all have bits of our body that we don't like. Often, we stress about things others don't even notice. Cracking these areas will help you feel good about yourself, which is the next part of solving the puzzle to look good and feel fantastic.

It all comes down to the number three. You can thank the Greek Philosopher Pythagoras for this, as he believed that the meaning behind numbers was profoundly significant. In his eyes, the number three was considered perfect, representing harmony, wisdom and understanding.

Three is a number used for visual effect – think of plants in the garden in groups of three. Have you ever noticed that shop displays usually have three items in total in the display or just three of each garment, like a jumper folded on a shelf?

Thinking in threes will help you get maximum effect when we look at outfit building or layering. Start with your lower half and choose a skirt, trousers, or jeans, then add a coordinating top before an overlayer like a shirt, jumper or jacket and voila!

Dressing well is about optical illusions. Balancing out your proportions using the 'Rule of Thirds' will help trick the eye into focusing away from certain areas and deceive the eye into seeing things differently from how they really are. Don't get me wrong – if you are a size 20, I can't make you look like a size 12 and if you are 5ft tall, I can't make you 5ft 8", but there are subtle things you can do that will help to tweak how the eye sees your silhouette.

Remember, the 'Rule of Thirds' is about splitting your body head to toe into three different areas – one line falls across your shoulders, another across your waist and the third line crosses your ankles. This enables you to see whether your body is long, and you have shorter legs proportionally or whether your legs are long, and you have a shorter body so that you can deceive the eye into balancing out your proportions.

If you have shorter legs and a long body, opting for high-waisted trousers/jeans or skirts gives the illusion that your waist is placed higher on the body than it actually is, making your body look shorter and your legs longer.

If you have longer legs and a shorter body, then choosing lower-dropped waist hemlines will give the illusion that your waist finishes lower down than it actually does, suggesting that your body is longer and your legs are shorter; however, how low you go with the waistline to flatter other aspects of your silhouette will depend on your body shape.

The key thing to remember is that to disguise your problem areas, you need to make your eyes look somewhere else instead.

Colour choice and where you place colour on the body play a big part; as a general rule, darker and plain colours help to hide, and brighter colours or patterns help to enhance.

Suppose you are someone with small boobs that you may want to enhance. In that case, it partly comes down to your choice of underwear, which we will cover in another chapter. You also want to divert the eye towards this area by choosing tops or jumpers with detail; light, bright colours or patterns will help. Avoid wearing low-cut, dark-coloured tops, as they will make your boobs look smaller.

Perhaps you are boobilicious but want to tone them down a bit and again, underwear choice will play a key part. 'V' necks and dark colours, especially non-patterned items worn on your top half, will help to minimise them. Anything with an open collar or a loose jacket/top is an excellent option, as the eye is drawn across to the shoulders and away from the boob area. Avoid wearing high necklines, tight tops and wide belts, as they will make your boobs look bigger.

Many people are not happy with their arms. As we age, those muscles that were once in use all the time can decide that they've given up and start to develop into "bingo wings". If you want to hide these, a batwing sleeve shape is a good option, as it will give you comfort without feeling constrained. Large wide scarves, pashminas or cardigans in smooth, floaty or sheer fabrics are a good option, too.

If you want to slim the appearance of your arms but still have a more structured top or jacket, then shoulder pads are the way forward as these "lift" the top of your arms, making them look longer. A good option – especially for wearing under knitwear, is to buy a base layer, such as a T-shirt containing shoulder pads. This will also improve your silhouette if you have rounded shoulders.

Avoid wearing tops with too tight or overly full sleeves, like puff sleeves. Also, avoid the tendency to opt for sleeveless tops/dresses – they may feel comfortable but will make your arms look thicker than they are.

If your tummy area or "muffin top" concerns you, wear soft draping fabrics, especially in wrap or blouson style tops with lower necklines to draw the eye away from your middle. Something with an all-over print or pattern will cleverly disguise a problem area as the eye sees the pattern as a whole rather than focusing on a specific point. Avoid clingy fabrics and straight styles, as they draw attention to your tummy.

If you have a more athletic frame and want to create the illusion of curves, anything containing ruffles, pleats or embellishments like sequins will add interest to your outfit. Thicker fabrics will add volume, and a belt can help to create a waistline to define your shape. Avoid wearing baggy, shapeless garments, as this can drown your silhouette.

An 'A' line dress or skirt will skim over a fuller, larger bottom without drawing attention to it. Bootleg trousers or jeans without pockets on the rear will also help visually slim your bottom area. Stick to darker colours below the waist and avoid wearing colours below the waist that are lighter or brighter than those above your waist, as the eye naturally looks to the brighter, lighter areas first.

If you want to look like your thighs are slimmer than they are, creating some volume in the clothes you wear on your upper body will help balance out your shape. 'A' line skirts and straight-leg trousers will skim your thighs. Trousers or jeans with a stripe or piping down the side seams will also help draw the eye away and elongate your legs. Avoid wearing shiny fabrics with patterns and detail on your lower body, as these will draw the eye towards your thighs, making them appear larger.

To look taller than you really are, the footwear you choose will play a part, which we will look at in a later chapter. You need to create the illusion of a vertical line to give the impression of a longer body and legs to look taller. Tonal dressing is a good choice here, as it is all about wearing a single colour (or very similar shades of that colour) head to toe. Choosing footwear in the same colour as bootleg jeans or trousers is a good option as it stops the eye from looking at your ankle area and gives the impression of longer legs.

Avoid wearing more than three colours at once, as this will only break up how the eye sees your body and make you look shorter.

Homework

Look in the mirror to see where your three lines are (across shoulders, waist and ankles) to ascertain whether you have a longer body and shorter legs or longer legs and a shorter body. This will help you with the positioning of waistlines and hemlines so that you choose garments to flatter your overall silhouette. If it helps, take a full-length selfie to refer to.

Look at the pieces in your wardrobe – your favourites and those you haven't worn in a while or still have tags attached. Try them on in front of the mirror, considering the advice contained in this chapter for enhancing/hiding your problem areas. If you feel good when you try it on, it's a keeper – if you aren't sure or don't like how the item fits or looks, it's time to say goodbye to it.

ANGELA YORKE

Chapter 6

Getting the Fit That Flatters

"I wanted to give a woman comfortable clothes that would flow with her body..."

Coco Chanel

Now that you have channelled your inner magician/illusionist, it helps to know a little about why things are placed where they are on garments and what they do to the silhouette that they create on you, as this will help you understand why specific garments work on some people and not others.

There's a bit of terminology involved, which can be especially useful when looking at garment descriptions when online shopping, where you don't have the opportunity to try the garments before you buy them. Once you know what things work for you, clothes shopping will be much quicker and easier as you will instantly know which pieces are worth trying and which will not work for your body shape.

Dress/Skirt Lengths

Mini skirt lengths can finish anywhere between the hip and knee, so the trick here is returning to the rule of thirds to find that sweet spot where the hemline will even out your silhouette. Some people love minis, and some people hate them – it's all a matter of personal choice and how you feel about wearing this style. If you feel good, then go for it! A mini length is not just for summer. Adding wool or opaque tights and a pair of heeled boots will also help you wear a mini length throughout the cooler months of the year.

Knee lengths can finish just above, on or slightly below the knee, so the length you choose that flatters you the most will once again come down to the rule of thirds and how you feel about showing off your legs/knees. The main thing is to look in the mirror and think about how you feel. If you have any doubts, you won't wear the item, so a different length may be a better choice.

A midi length traditionally finishes around the calf. If you are sporty and have enhanced calf muscles, this may not be the best look for you, as it will draw the eye to your calf area. It can sometimes look a little frumpy if not styled well. Opting for fabrics that move well at this hemline is key as this keeps the look fluid without overly emphasising your calf muscles. A different hemline will be more flattering if you prefer a stiffer fabric like a wool skirt or heavy cotton.

A-Line is a design shape that follows the shape of a letter 'A', where the point of the 'A' is at your waist and graduates outwards. This is a flattering cut for most people, as it skims over the hips to balance out your body shape, looking especially good when the fabric used is not too stiff.

Maxi lengths usually finish at the ankle or even down to the floor in some cases, so your choice of footwear will be especially key if you don't want to trip up or risk damaging your item.

Sleeves

There are many different types of sleeves out there that work in various ways depending on your body shape. The main thing to remember is that the eye will be drawn to the point where the sleeve ends, so this is something to think about when considering the parts of your body that you may want to show off or hide away. Don't worry if the sleeve lengths on tops do not finish where you want them to. If you like the top and feel-good wearing it, you can still wear it – the aim is to feel good and look good, too. You could consider wearing it as a layering piece, either under or over a different sleeve length, to get the overall look you want.

A dropped sleeve is where the hemline of the sleeve at the shoulder doesn't actually sit on the shoulder and sits slightly lower down on the upper arm. This shape gives extra room around the armpit area and is very comfortable.

A batwing sleeve is sometimes paired with a dropped sleeve. This is a wide sleeve forming a triangle shape from the waist to the shoulder area, making it a good option for hiding 'bingo wings.' It is also a style that works well if you have larger boobs, as it can help even out your silhouette and draw attention away from them (if that is what you want to do).

A cap sleeve is a short sleeve that covers your shoulders and over onto the top of the arm. It is not just a good option for a warm day; it is a way of drawing attention towards your face and neck and away from other problem areas.

A butterfly sleeve finishes midway between the shoulder and elbow. It is usually made from a generous amount of flowing fabric so that it drapes like a butterfly's wings. It's often a favourite for lace sleeves or satin-type fabrics.

A puff sleeve is, as the name suggests... a bit puffy. There will be volume in the sleeve material along the arm, which then gathers in at the hemline of the sleeve. It's great for adding drama to a look and drawing attention up and away from your lower half.

A raglan sleeve can often be found on baseball-style T-shirts featuring two colours. The sleeves are diagonally joined over the shoulder in a contrasting colour which draws the eye towards the neckline and away from other areas.

A leg of mutton sleeve is similar to a puff sleeve. However, the volume of fabric will usually stop at the elbow, and the elbow-to-wrist part of the garment will be more fitted in style – often featuring covered buttons in a row down towards the wrist. This is another excellent option for adding drama to an outfit.

Elbow-length sleeves draw the attention of the eye towards your waistline. This is an excellent sleeve choice to show off your waist and works incredibly well if your outfit has a decorative belt attached, too.

¾ sleeves are not just great for doing the washing up. (i.e. they don't dangle in the water). If you like pushing your sleeves up to expose a bit of skin on the arm, these will be a good option. Very useful for layering beneath other longer-sleeved pieces and a good choice for petites. Be careful if you have extra-long arms, as the sleeve length will give the impression that your arms are longer.

Long sleeves will either finish around the bone of your wrist or go to a full-length finish at the back of your hand, depending on the garment's cut. Long sleeves are a classic look that works well for everyone. If you have long arms and feel that the sleeve sits a bit shorter than you would like, then opt for bracelets to fill the gap – the kind of bracelets that come in sets of thin metal bangles where all are the same will look great when worn together helping to plug the shortfall.

Coats

You need to consider what you are wearing beneath a coat – it's not just a case of grabbing a coat and chucking it on.

If you sometimes find that the sleeves of a tailored style of coat seem a little short, this is because traditionally, the sleeves on a coat were designed to finish at the bone of your wrist, with the idea being that the cuff of your shirt/blouse beneath would be shown or the jewellery on your wrist.

Aim to match the hemline of a dress or skirt to the hemline of your coat when balancing out your overall silhouette. You may wear a calf-length skirt with an ankle-length coat. However, there is an imbalance in the hems, making the overall look not quite right unless the colours of both garments are very similar.

Jackets that finish at waist length will be fine with a longer-line dress or skirt and look great with trousers or jeans.

A knee-length coat or a maxi-length coat will work fantastically with trousers. As your legs are covered up, there is no issue with the rule of thirds. Your overall silhouette will work, especially if you wear the coat open.

Leg Lengths and Shapes

Gone are the days when there were just a handful of shapes to choose from. Not only do we have a myriad of natural and manufactured fabrics that impact how a leg shape looks, but a myriad of leg styles and shapes, too - especially when buying jeans or a smart/casual trouser.

A cropped style will finish below the mid-calf area and vary in length to the ankle. Sometimes, this style can be called an ankle skimmer. Finding the right cropped length that flatters you will be a matter of trial and error, depending on your height, how long your legs are and how well-defined your calves are.

A capri cut is shorter than a cropped cut as the leg length ends higher than the mid-calf area. This fitted or tapered leg is usually made from cotton, linen or natural fabrics. It's a classic shape for a smart/casual look – think Audrey Hepburn and 1950s styles.

A cigarette cut is a skinny cut that will hug your thighs and hips. As the name suggests, it runs straight down from the knee to the hem at the ankle. A slightly wider leg opening allows the hemline to cover your shoes and is a great option to wear with heels if you want to elongate the look of your legs.

A sailor style is inspired by nautical designs of the past and is easily identified by a row of buttons over the front of the hips on each side and a slightly flared cut to the leg.

A paper bag style has a very distinctive look as the waistline of the trousers is usually ruffled – looking like you have scrunched together a paper bag in your hand. There is usually an inbuilt belt made from the same fabric as the rest of the garment. This will not be a good option if you carry weight around your middle, given the extra fabric gathered at the waist area. This style looks fantastic on petites.

Wide-leg trousers that flare from the thighs look great with shorter jackets that finish at the waist. Flat or chunky shoes, especially a platform trainer, will also work well with this style, as they balance out your look. They are called wide legs as they are a wide cut at the thigh and bottom area and start to flare around the mid-thigh area, giving a more triangular shape to your silhouette.

A skinny fit is usually made from a material with a lot of stretch. These fit your shape quite tightly, showing off all your shape in your hips, thighs, legs, and bottom. It suits an athletic H body shape and an X hourglass shape and is a good choice for petites as the cut enhances the leg length in your silhouette.

A straight cut is considered an original classic. It is tighter on the thighs, slightly looser at the ankles and calf areas and suits most body shapes.

A regular fit goes straight down from your hips to your thighs and follows the shape of your body more closely than a straight cut. It also tends to be narrower at the ankles.

A relaxed fit is similar to a regular fit but a bit more oversized, so it is looser in the bottom and thigh area for comfort.

A loose fit is a generous cut that fits loosely over the bottom, thighs, hips and calves, with loose ankles rather than being fitted.

A boyfriend cut will fit perfectly around your hips and waist with a looser fit over the legs. This style is very comfortable and especially good when travelling.

A girlfriend cut is very similar to a boyfriend cut, just a slightly slimmer version and not as baggy, which suits a curvy body shape.

A bootcut is, as the name suggests, perfect for wearing over boots as the leg tapers slightly from the knee to drape over your boot but without being too flared. This style tends to be more fitted over the thighs and bottom and is excellent for everyone to wear, especially if you are curvy.

A flare cut is that iconic 70's style that is tight on the thigh and bottom and then tapers down to be very wide at the bottom hem over your shoe. This style looks great on taller physiques but can drown a petite silhouette. Curvy body shapes, apple and A shapes look fab in this type of cut. Ideally, wear a platform trainer or chunky shoes to balance out the look.

Pockets

Italian pockets are the horizontal slanted pockets that are often seen in the trousers of tailored menswear. They show as a "slit" on the outside with all the pocket fabric on the inside of the garment. This style works well for athletic H body shapes. If you are curvy over the hips, the pockets will bend outwards and not sit flat which draws attention to your hips, making them look more prominent. One way around this is to stitch the pockets closed so that they are no longer functional pockets and will not bend open when you move; however, if the fabric of the garment is thick or it is a very fitted style, then this may be uncomfortable to wear.

Welt pockets are usable pockets that look like slits in the garment. They are very low-key, discreet and a great option as they don't add any bulk to the garment. They are usually placed strategically to divert the eye to a particular area or enhance a garment's detail. Often there may be detailed embroidery around the "slit" of the pocket or embellishments.

Patch pockets are what they say, they can be made from the same material or contrasting material/colour and sewn onto the garment to add detail without volume. The placement of the pocket can do different things to your silhouette as the eye is drawn to the location of the pocket. If it is a blouse with pockets over the boob area and you are conscious of your boobs, then you may prefer to go for a blouse that doesn't have pockets on the front. This type of pocket is often seen on the bottom area of jeans and can be any shape.

Flap pockets are pockets with a flap over and sometimes a fastener like a popper or button. Some jeans feature this type of pocket on the rear. The extra fabric flap will draw attention to your rear. It can make your bottom look more prominent, so if you are large-bottomed and want to play this down, avoid jeans with flap pockets.

Inverted pleat pockets are similar to a flap pocket but have a pleat down the middle. They are often featured in workwear styles like cargo trousers or safari-style jackets. These are usable pockets that expand, so the placement of the pocket on the garment is key. If this type of pocket is on the thigh of a cargo trouser, it will draw the eye to that point, so this is something to think about if you have larger thighs that you want to hide.

Faux pockets are fake pockets designed for the garment's attractiveness and not for practical use. Usually, it is just the outer pocket detail attached to the garment; however, a tiny interior space may sometimes feature. It all depends on the fabric and design of the garment. Again, the eye will be directed to where the faux pockets sit on the garment, so this is something to consider carefully, depending on whether you want to hide or enhance the area.

Jacket lengths

Chanel-style jackets are a boxy, iconic shape that finishes just below the waist. This is very flattering for most body shapes and a great choice to lengthen your silhouette, giving the impression of long legs.

Some jackets or blazers traditionally finish mid-hip length, which can hide your body if you carry weight around your middle; however, if you are a curvy shape over the hips, you should wear the jacket/blazer open and not buttoned up.

Longer line jackets will finish at the top of the thigh, which looks great if you have a more athletic H body shape; however, if you carry your weight on your hips and thighs, it will probably finish at your widest point and not be a flattering look.

I am sure that at some point, everyone has seen a garment that they absolutely love. It doesn't quite fit right, but you love it and buy it intending to get it altered...then it sits in the wardrobe with the tag on, and you never get that alteration done.

Getting an alteration made to a garment to tailor the fit to yourself can be a great idea; however, you need to consider what the garment is, the type of fabric involved and the pattern details or embellishments on the garment.

Leg lengths, in particular, have traditionally been cut and taken up if you need to shorten them - I remember standing on a chair with my Mum pinning up the hem before taking a pair of scissors to cut off the excess and sewing a new hem. However, this does ruin the line of the leg and the shape at the bottom of the leg; therefore, if taking up trouser leg lengths, you need to keep the original hem ending and reattach it to the leg so that the seams are all still in the right place for best effect. It is not too much of a problem if you are taking up an item of plain clothing; however, if your garment has a print, you need to match up the print, which can make the alteration tricky, costly and time-consuming.

Alterations don't just have to remove fabric from a garment; they can add fabric instead. I have a tall work colleague who loved a particular jumpsuit that fitted her body shape and was really comfortable but too short in the leg, so she added a complimentary fabric to the hem of the leg to make it look longer and it looked fantastic.

For a tailored coat that may have become too tight in the arms, it is possible to undo the sleeve seam and add a panel of similar (or contrasting) fabric that sits beneath the arm to widen the sleeves and give you more longevity from your coat. This is particularly worth considering if it is an item of sentimental value you can't part with and would ideally still like to wear.

Unfortunately, for many alterations (apart from leg lengths), you may find that having made the alteration, it still doesn't quite work for you, so you do need to weigh up the costs of having the alterations made and whether you will actually wear the garment, otherwise it may be a better idea to walk away from that piece and invest in something else that will work better for your shape.

Homework

Really get to know what parts of your body you want to hide (if any) and which parts you want to show off.

Consider the hemlines on your coats, jackets, skirts and dresses and evaluate if these sit in places that flatter your silhouette.

Take a fresh look at the garments in your wardrobe to see where pockets are placed and look at the sleeves of your garments to see if they work for you.

If you love something but it isn't quite right, consider whether the item can be altered to fit and whether it is cost-effective before proceeding.

Chapter 7

Building the Right Foundations

"When it comes to underwear, there's nothing worse than a visible panty line."

Brad Goreski

The art of dressing well is not limited to getting the proper fit of clothes to suit your body shape; you need to get your foundations right too.

We all know that a house built with poor foundations is prone to sagging; the same applies to what you wear beneath your clothing. The foundations are essentially your underwear and your whole look can be enhanced or ruined if you get these basics wrong.

You may remember back in the 1990s, style gurus Trinny Woodall and Gok Wan were huge advocates of this, especially when it came to bras.

The starting point is to wear the right underwear for your outfit – not just the correct type of knickers to avoid a VPL (visible pant line), which can ruin your silhouette, but get the right colour of underwear, too. Let's face it – those sexy black undies may make you feel fantastic, but it's not the best idea to wear them under a white outfit...unless you are trying to show off your ass..ets!

Neutral-coloured underwear in flimsy "second skin" style breathable fabrics are a good option. The neutral shade will mean that whatever you wear it with, you won't have to worry about colours showing through fabrics. The "second skin" thin fabric also sits closer to your skin and avoids bulking out at the hems, which is the cause of the VPL.

If you wear flowing fabrics and rarely wear anything fitted below the waist, then the style of your knickers will be less of a concern; however, if you like to wear a tighter fit of trousers over the hips or a skinny jean, then you need to pay attention to where the hemlines of your underwear finish.

If you have something to wear that is quite a snug fit and lumps and bumps to even out, consider investing in some waist-high super skimming "Bridget Jones" knickers. They may not be the most sexy-looking things in their own right, but they help smooth body lines beneath your outfit, giving you more confidence when you look in the mirror.

Similarly, body-shaping underwear can be bought to help hold in tummies, smoothing things if you carry weight around your middle. Some are "corset style", some are attached to the knickers, and some have a swimsuit style body. When it comes to choosing the right one for you, it will come down to personal preference as well as the outfit you intend to wear over it.

While not technically underwear, if you have rounded shoulders, investing in a base layer T-shirt with soft shoulder pads will help square the line of your shoulders so that sleeves hang better, and your overall silhouette is improved. We're not talking about 1980s power shoulder pads, just soft, subtle shoulder pads in the T-shirt. Wearing this beneath a jumper, for example, will also help with the illusion that you are a little taller as the eye is drawn straight across the shoulders rather than to the slope of the shoulder. Zara is a retailer that usually carries stock of shoulder-padded T-shirts at a relatively low cost, but I am sure there are others.

Did you know that most women (over 85%) wear the wrong bra size? This means they are often uncomfortable or, in many cases, feel sore or in pain. Even worse, many women wear the same bra for over five years.

Many women don't take the time or trouble to get themselves measured. They often guess which size they should wear, which is tricky when bra sizes vary between brands. It can be hard to find a bra that feels comfortable, and when we do, quite often we stick with it until sometimes it's older than our children are. Bras have a lifespan; the longer you stick with them, the more you wash them, and their support deteriorates as the elastic and elastane contained in the fabric will gradually stretch. Refreshing your bra supplies and having a regular bra fitting is a good idea, as our bodies usually change their shape over time depending on our age and lifestyles.

If you are a sporty type – especially someone who runs or jogs, please invest in a good quality sports bra. I have seen so many women, looking very uncomfortable with their boobs bouncing in all sorts of directions. It's not just a visual thing; your boobs are precious assets and all that unnecessary bouncing around is going to affect the muscle strength behind and lead to sagging boobs. By restraining them properly for exercise, not only are you protecting them, but you will probably find that exercising becomes a little more comfortable and possibly more enjoyable, too.

A proper bra fitting with an independent bra fitter or shop is a necessity. Most offer fittings as a free service or for a small fee that is redeemable against the cost of a purchase. It is worth investing a little more money when buying a new bra – like most things – you get what you pay for. Typically, a mass-produced bra may be cheaper but will have fewer components to it, which means it can be made in about three minutes.

A quality bra has many more elements that help with fit and sizing. It takes around an hour to produce, so it will ultimately give you more support in all the right places, making your silhouette look slimmer, too.

A bra fitter can assist you to get the right style and fit for the kind of support that you need, irrespective of how big or small your boobs are. Nobody wants to look or feel like their boobs are resting on their stomach and your outfit will thank you for the proper support to help it hang beautifully on your body. If you are big-boobed, a correctly fitted bra can help to reduce back pain as well as help with your general posture.

A strapless bra is necessary if you like to wear strapless garments or those with thin straps. Some bras can be bought with interchangeable straps giving a clear strap option which can be handy if you are bigger boobed and feel that strapless is not an option for you. The clear strap or strapless option is a good choice if you wear a top with lace panelling across the shoulders, as this avoids having a visible bra strap spoiling the effect of the lace detail in the garment.

A soft-shell smooth cup without lace detailing will work best under T-shirts or delicate fabrics like satin or silk. Bras with lace detailing can make the appearance of a T-shirt or a flimsy fabric look bumpy, so a soft-shell version will help give a smoother line.

A common issue with bra straps, in general, is that they often don't sit where you want them to for the cut of the tops that you wear. If you have a racerback or tank top, consider getting an adjuster for your strap. They can usually be bought cheaply in either black, white or nude shades and sometimes as a pack of all three. They hook your straps together in the middle of your back so that your straps are hidden from view and don't spoil the effect of the outfit.

Whilst we are talking boobs, it's also important to talk about regularly checking yourself for any signs of changes in the boob area. Checking for puckering, inverted nipples, discharge or feeling for any unusual lumps or bumps is vital in the bid to beat breast cancer. Check out Breast Cancer Now or Coppafeel Breast Cancer Charity websites for the most up-to-date information on how to check yourself regularly and for new developments in the bid to beat breast cancer. If anything has changed or you have concerns, immediately contact your GP for further advice.

Homework

Review your underwear drawer – discard anything that has seen better days and lost its stretch.

Book a bra fitting at your local independent bra shop to get the right style and support for your size.

Consider what type of bra/straps you need for the items you regularly wear and invest in a strap adjuster if you wear racerback styles.

A good quality sports bra is essential if you have an active lifestyle.

Time to check how old your bras are. You should change your bra every six months, but if you look after bras using a washing net when washing, they should last a little longer.

Visit Breast Cancer Now or Coppafeel Breast Cancer charity websites for the most up-to-date information and check your boobs. Immediately contact your GP for any changes or anything that concerns you.

Chapter 8

20/20 Wardrobe Vision

"I knew who I was this morning, but I've changed a few times since then."

Lewis Carroll

Ok, it's time to tackle the elephant in the room – i.e. your wardrobe.

Most people have a wardrobe bulging at the seams, crammed with items to the point that you may have forgotten what is in there if you cannot see it. Over time, we gradually add pieces to our wardrobe, accumulating things slowly to the point where everything gets out of hand.

Before we go any further on this journey, take a good, long look at what you already have and make some decisions. It's not a quick fix process as there are probably things squirrelled away in there that you are emotionally attached to.

At the start of the book, I mentioned that the items in your wardrobe need to reflect the lifestyle you lead. There's no point having 10 cocktail dresses if you haven't needed to wear one in the last 20 years!

Most people find that they regularly wear only 20% of their wardrobe items, and some may wear even less. If you think about the items you wear day in and day out, you probably have a generic "uniform"; for example, if you are a busy Mum, you may spend most of your time in jeans that you dress down when with the children or dress up with a smarter top/jacket and heels if you can get a babysitter and get out.

Before you start your wardrobe declutter, you need to consider the following things.

- Time – this isn't a quick process and will probably take a few hours of uninterrupted time. However long you think it's going to take, I suggest you double it! Once you start, you are in the thick of the process, so think about when you can dedicate uninterrupted time to do this; otherwise, you will find that everything goes back in the wardrobe until another day, and you won't have achieved anything.

- Get organised – I recommend being prepared with six differently labelled boxes (or bags). Labels are essential so that as you go through everything, you can "file" it into the appropriate "to-do" piles which, without a label, can become mixed up along the way.

  - Box 1 to keep and put back in your wardrobe later.

  - Box 2 to keep but store elsewhere as you may wear it for special occasions (like a wedding), or it may be an item you are emotionally attached to and don't want to part with.

- Box 3 to sell on so that you can recoup some cash to reinvest in key pieces that you may be missing or to replace damaged items.

- Box 4 to pass on to a friend, your local charity shop or donate to a clothing bank (often found in the carparks of large supermarkets).

- Box 5 for damaged/stained items that need to be disposed of.

- Box 6 items you want to keep that can be repaired or repurposed into something else.

You will find it easier to tackle this as one big task, but if you really can't face that (or think it will take you a few days as you have a vast wardrobe space and haven't decluttered it since 1989) then tackle a particular section of your wardrobe at a time (like your T-shirt pile) before revisiting the exercise as a whole when it is more manageable.

The first step is to take everything out of your wardrobe so that it is empty...and be amazed that you had managed to cram that much stuff in there in the first place.

Whilst your wardrobe is empty, I recommend you clean it as it's one of those places that often gets overlooked. Make the most of this opportunity - not only will your wardrobe smell lovely, but there is less chance of bugs laying eggs on your clothing and eating holes in the fabric!

Invest in some lavender (or other essential oil) bags that hang from your clothes hangers, as this will help to keep bugs away and protect your clothing. These can often be found at your local Craft Fairs or Makers Markets. If you buy from there rather than immediately going online, you will be supporting a local small business or good cause with your purchase.

Next comes the hard part. For each item, you need to decide which box it falls into.

Hold up each garment in front of a mirror (or, better still, try it on) and take a good hard look at it.

- Does it fit you? It must leave your wardrobe if it's too small or too big.

- Is it stained, ripped, damaged or broken? If so, it must leave your wardrobe to be repaired, repurposed or disposed of.

- Does the colour suit you? Does it make your eyes sparkle and your skin brighten? If not, it may be the wrong shade for you, and you need to rethink.

- How long has it been since you last wore the item? If you haven't worn it in the previous two years, it is time to say goodbye to it from your wardrobe space.

- Does the shape of the garment suit you? Is it a piece that makes you feel good when you wear it?

- Does the garment fit your lifestyle? If not, it's time to leave your wardrobe space, either say goodbye to it or store it elsewhere.

- Is the garment right for your style personality? You may need to rethink if you don't like ruffles in your clothing and it has ruffles.

- If the garment has a bold print, when you look in the mirror, do you see the print first, or do you see yourself? I.e. Do you wear the print, or does the print wear you? If the latter, you may want to part company.

- Does the item look dated? Vintage garments are one thing, but some pieces can look "wrong" in the grand scheme of things. If you decide to say goodbye, it may be a piece to advertise in a vintage sale environment. If it is a genuine vintage item, consider a specialist sale to get the best price if you decide to sell it.

- Is the item of sentimental value meaning you don't want to wear or part with it? If so, it must leave your wardrobe to relocate to an alternative storage space.

- If the garment doesn't look right, but you still like it, can it be repurposed into something else? For example, a dress you love that doesn't fall at the right length could be adapted to become a blouse to wear with jeans or items in pretty fabrics could be repurposed into handmade coat hanger lavender bags.

- Does the item still have its original tags attached, and if so, can you actually remember when and why you bought it? This could have been a rash purchase because it was a "bargain" at the time, or you may have forgotten it was there.

- Does the item go with anything else in your wardrobe to create an outfit? If not, it's time to say goodbye unless you love the piece and intend to buy something to wear with it.

Once you have gone through everything in your wardrobe, take action with the contents of your boxes.

Start with Box 2, which is your storage box. Once these items are packed neatly in storage, you can focus on what is left.

Next, deal with Box 5 of your damaged/stained items that must be disposed of. Some local kerbside recycling schemes will take them if they are bagged up but check with your local Council website first.

Put Box 4 into your car boot containing everything for donating to your local charity shop or clothing bank. If you don't, then whilst it is in view, you may be tempted to go back into the box and pull things out to put them back into your wardrobe.

Consider how you want to sell on the contents of Box 3. There may be a local dress agency near where you live that will take a commission selling the items on your behalf or consider using an online selling facility like eBay or Vinted. Alternatively, your local Facebook Marketplace may be a source for selling your items without paying a commission. Depending on the time of year, you may consider taking them to a car boot sale. There are Swish Shopping Events in some areas, and some larger clothing retailers occasionally organise them, too. A Swish is a clothes swap event where however many pieces you take in, you can bring home the same number of pieces. It's an enjoyable event – especially if you go with a friend. However, you need to be careful not to swap items just for the sake of it. If you decide to go, stick to swapping your items for things that you need or that will complement the outfits you already have. You need to have a plan and stick to it.

Box 6 contains items you want to keep that can be repaired or repurposed into something else. This needs to be put aside where you will see and act on it. Don't store it back in the base of your wardrobe, or you will never get around to doing anything with the contents. The legs of jeans/trousers that are in good condition can be cut and made into little handy make-up bags; cotton or viscose items can be cut into heart, circular or square shapes with an offcut of ribbon attached to make into wardrobe hanger lavender sachets and lovely lightweight fabrics can be cut into large squares to use as an alternative form of wrapping paper – this is a good way for repurposing sari materials or materials with some sparkle or metallic threads that can fold easily without stiffness in the fabric.

The items inside Box 1 that you want to keep and put back in your wardrobe should be checked over to see if they need any TLC – e.g. jumpers may need to be de-bobbled with a cashmere comb or run a lint roller over jackets that may have picked up fluff/hair along the way or there may be pieces that need some spot cleaning or washing to spruce them up.

The next chapter will give tips and tricks for storing your garments for tidiness, longevity and visual appeal so you can see what you have when you open your wardrobe.

Homework

Find six large boxes or large bags to use for your sort-out. Plastic storage boxes with lids are ideal if you have them, but bin bags will work equally well for this.

You need six large pieces of paper to write your box/bag labels so that you know which box contains which things, as it is easy to get them mixed up along the way.

Plan the time in your diary to declutter your wardrobe when you are unlikely to be disturbed. If you know you will be interrupted or cannot finish this in one go, make sure you can leave everything where it is until you can get back to it without having to stick it all back in the wardrobe again.

Chapter 9
Storage Tips and Tricks

"Would you tell me, please,
which way I ought to go from here?"
Lewis Carroll

After completing your sort-out, it's time to think about how you store your garments rather than just sticking them back in the wardrobe 'willy nilly'. You need to be able to see what you have to create your outfits and if you can't see the wood for the trees, you will quickly sink back into old habits.

It's not just hanging your garments but also how you store other items that need consideration so that you can see what you have when putting your outfits together. Taking care of how you store your clothing makes it look tidier and visually appealing. It also protects the fibres in your clothes so that they last longer. After all, they are an investment whether an item was bought for £5 or £500.

Before you rush out to your nearest store or Amazon, it's important to remember that storage doesn't have to be expensive. Re-using boxes that you already have can sometimes fit the bill, especially things like empty shoe boxes or gift box packaging, depending on what you are storing.

The starting point is to ensure you have decent coat hangers to hang garments in your wardrobe. The velvet-covered slim hangers that can be bought in supermarkets are a good investment. The velvet covering stops delicate clothes from sliding off the hanger and holds things in place. Being slim also means you can fit more items into your wardrobe; however, I recommend a chunky or padded hanger for jackets and coats to keep the shoulders shaped.

Coat hanger hooks are a good low-cost investment. These small plastic v-shaped pieces slide over the top of your coat hanger so that you can attach another coat hanger to it. Alternatively, a ring pull from a canned drink works equally well. These can hang items vertically in your wardrobe, giving you more space on your rail. You can buy metal bar hangers with a hook at each end that does a similar job. However, the metal hooks can damage or tear other items in the wardrobe as they can be pretty sharp.

When considering how to store your clothes, it comes down to personal choice. Some people like to store their items in outfits, so they are ready to take them out of the wardrobe without thinking about them too much when deciding what to wear in the morning.

Others like to store items by colour, e.g. all black items together, all red items together, etc., or you can store your items by garment type – storing all tops together, all trousers together, or all jackets together, etc. It all depends on what works for you. The key is to see what is in there and avoid duplicating items or "losing" items that you forget about to the back of the wardrobe again.

Some items, such as knitwear, should not be stored on a coat hanger and needs to be folded. Storing knitwear on a hanger will distort the shape of the knit and can lead to bumps appearing in the wrong places around the shoulder. The weight of the knit can also stretch your garment out of shape or get caught on the buttons or zips of other clothes in your wardrobe, which can lead to snagging. Knitwear can be stored folded over the lower part of a coat hanger, but this does take up a lot of room, so ideally, folding or rolling to store on a shelf is the way to go.

Jeans are another piece that can be hung in the wardrobe, but I much prefer to store them folded on a shelf. You can do this in two ways to avoid them toppling all over the place, like the Leaning Tower of Pisa, one of which will keep the fold intact even if you pick them up by the waistband after folding.

The first technique is to lay the jeans out flat on the floor with the back pockets facing upwards and then fold them so that the legs are long and together with the crotch of the jeans folded inwards to make a straight rectangular line to the jeans. Place one hand where the crotch of the jeans is and fold the hips and waist over your hand. Next, take the ankle hem of the leg and fold it into the waist of the jeans to create a pocket.

The second way of folding your jeans is to lay them flat on the floor, then take one leg and fold it so that the hem of the leg is level with the jeans' waistband. Next, fold the short leg over onto the long leg, then take the hem of the longer leg and fold it upwards to touch the first fold (so you still have one leg longer than the other). Then, fold it over again and fold the waistband back over to form a compact square-ish shape. This is an excellent option if you have jeans of different lengths, as they are all now the same shape after folding and will stack neatly on a shelf.

If you don't want to fold your jeans and prefer to hang them, then fold them long so that you have a long rectangular shape and slip the jean belt loops over the hanger's hook. You can then fold the leg over the coat hanger, or you can leave them to dangle.

If you want to store T-shirts or tops so that they neatly stack and are all the same shape after folding, use an old kitchen chopping board or part of an old cardboard box that is the size of the space you want your garment to sit in. Place the board behind the neck of the top and fold each arm and side of the garment over the box before folding up the lower hem of the garment. Remove the board and move on to the next item for folding and all of your garments will be folded to the same size.

Accessories can be stored together. For belts, you can buy coat hangers with lots of hooks attached to the bottom so that you can slip the belt buckle onto the hook, storing around 10 belts on one hanger. Another option is to use a kitchen roll holder to stack belts vertically. I recommend rolling the belt on the inward side by pushing one end through the buckle from the outside before rolling up. This way, the belt will be reluctant to unravel after stacking.

Ikea has some great options for drawer dividers, which are not just suitable for separating underwear and socks. These can be handy for storing bracelets and lightweight scarves by folding and/or rolling the scarves. However, small boxes from packaging are just as good.

I like to use a metal grid panel with a hanger attached to the top for storing necklaces. The metal panel is divided into squares so you can fasten one or two necklaces into each square to avoid them getting tangled up. Alternatively, a wooden coat hanger with hooks screwed into the bottom can be used to hang belts or necklaces to prevent them getting tangled up.

Shoe storage is best done so you can see your shoes. If you have shoes that you don't wear very often – perhaps shoes that go with special occasion outfits that you would not otherwise wear daily then storing them in shoe boxes so that you can stack them is great. The rest of your shoes should ideally be stored in pairs on a shoe rack so that you can see what you have for putting outfits together.

Outfits of the special occasion kind, which only come out at Christmas or for occasional black-tie events, do not need to be hanging in sight in your wardrobe daily. Pop the items in garment covers before folding and storing them away from your wardrobe.

When I was younger, we were always encouraged to store away our winter woollies during summer and then swap over to store away our summer T-shirts during the winter. Undoubtedly, there will be a few high summer pieces and swimsuits – the sort of holiday packing pieces that can be stored away, but to get the most wear from your clothing, consider keeping all items in full view in your wardrobe. This will enable you to layer your outfits and have clothes that cross seasons. Overall, you will need fewer clothes as more pieces will work for you all year round as part of your capsule wardrobe.

Homework

Invest in some decent velvet-covered coat hangers for your wardrobe. Have all of your coat hangers the same for maximum storage.

If you want to store outfits together, invest in coat hanger hooks to slip over the hangers or use ring pulls from canned drinks instead.

Consider how you want to organise your wardrobe — is it by outfit colour or type of garment?

Take time to fold your garments using the techniques described to maximise your storage capacity.

Store away "special occasion" outfits so they are not hanging in your day-to-day wardrobe. This space should be reserved for the pieces that you wear daily.

Chapter 10
Fabric Decoder and Laundry Guide

*"Take care of your costume and
your confidence will take care of itself."*
Amit Kalantri

Many new fabric types are being developed for broader use in clothing production.

All fabric types can be classed as one of two things: natural fabrics from things that grow, or manufactured fabrics. Sometimes, different fabrics are combined to construct a garment to offer different qualities, such as breathability or comfort. There are pros and cons to all types of fabrics; some need more looking after than others.

Polyester is a synthetic, plastic-based fibre. With growing awareness of eco issues, new polyester garments are often crafted from recycled waste polyester or plastic water bottles. Gone are the days of horrible polyester full of static, giving you electric shocks and making your hair stand on end! Today's polyester is usually super soft and can sometimes feel like silk. Look for high-quality polyester garments, as the saying "you get what you pay for" is valid for this fabric.

Econyl is a fabric made from recycled Nylon. It is produced by an Italian company that uses industrial plastic waste and fishing nets recovered from the sea. The result is a fabric that is just as good as newly manufactured Nylon.

Viscose is a popular fabric made from wood pulp. This makes the fabric soft and breathable - a "lifesaver" for menopausal hot flushes. It usually needs little or no ironing, provided you wash it on a slow spin cycle and hang it to dry on a coat hanger.

Tencel is a brand name for two sustainable fabrics made by an Austrian company. You may see them as Tencel Lyocell or Tencel Modal. Tencel is another fabric crafted from wood pulp, feeling like heavy silk.

Cotton is the fabric we probably know the most, crafted from the "fluff" harvested from the cotton plant. Soft, breathable and comfortable, it washes well and can usually be tumble-dried. Organic cotton options are available. However, all cotton fabrics use a lot of water in the growing process, so they are not great for the environment, and many producers are now creating recycled cotton fabrics to tackle this issue.

Hemp is related to the marijuana plant family and is often used for eco-friendly garments as it uses less water to grow than cotton. It's durable and becoming more popular and similar to cotton.

Bamboo Linen or Bamboo Lyocell are fabrics made from Bamboo pulp. Bamboo is growing in popularity due to its eco-credentials as a quick-growing sustainable plant. However, not all bamboo-mixed fabrics are good for the environment.

With the increasing popularity of vegan lifestyles, fabrics are adapting to meet consumer needs, especially when creating faux leather alternatives that are not PVC-based. The bark from cork trees is sometimes used to make a washable faux leather material.

Pinatex is the name of a vegan leather made from pineapple leaves that would otherwise go to waste after the pineapple harvest each year and some vegan leather alternatives can be made using mangoes (who knew?).

Linen is often used in sustainable fashion, as linen flax needs less water to grow than the cotton plant. It's a quick-drying, breathable fabric perfect for warmer climates, but you must look after it. Linen is one of the oldest known fabrics used to make clothing since the Pharaohs in Egypt.

Many summer outfits feature beautiful pieces of linen clothing, but it can be a tricky thing to look after. You may have bought a gorgeous top or beautiful linen trousers, worn once, then hung up only to find it full of creases. Maybe you have popped something linen into the wash and dried it outside on a sunny washing line for a little bit too long, only to find that your beautiful item now has laundry liquid "stripes" and the fabric is stiff, making it a nightmare to iron so you leave it at the bottom of the ironing pile until you next need to wear it. However, it stays there...and you wear something else instead! Sound familiar?

A laundry bag is a good investment for linen garments. Always use a cold wash on a delicate cycle with a short spin. Never tumble dry linen, as this will most likely cause shrinkage, so pop it on a hanger to dry. You will need to dry linen in the shade to avoid sun fading...unless you deliberately want a more washed-out colour to your garment.

Always hang your linen pieces in your wardrobe, as no matter how good you are at folding, there will inevitably be creases that you must deal with, which can be stubborn. Ideally, use a padded hanger for linen tops/jackets to avoid getting the hanger line across the shoulders. If you do have to fold, make sure you put your folded piece on top of a pile of other folded pieces to avoid compression creases – ideally, avoid the folding altogether and roll up your item instead, especially if you are packing it into a suitcase. When you reach your destination, unpack and hang up your linen items immediately so any creases can drop out. If you find that creases are stubborn, hang your item in the bathroom so that the steam from your shower or bath can help to relax the material's fibres helping the creases to drop out in their own time.

Ideally, don't iron your linen garments, as the heat and pressure from the iron can crush the fibres in the fabric if your iron is too hot. Steaming is a much better option, but if you feel you must iron, turn inside out and mist with a water sprayer first or iron whilst your garment is still slightly damp.

If you spill something on linen (or any other fabric), tackle it immediately. Don't wait for the stain to dry; it will be harder to remove after being absorbed into the fabric's fibres. Most of the time, a wipe with a damp cloth and a little detergent can do the trick. However, ensure you rinse off and pop in the wash as soon as possible to avoid a paler patch appearing where the stain once was. For stubborn stains, use a baking soda paste made from a bit of baking soda mixed with water to tackle your stain. Test the paste on an inside seam first to check that no fading occurs, then wash again. Don't iron over the spot where your stain was, as this will draw more attention to the area rather than hiding it.

At the end of the day, like a lovely comforting cup of hot chocolate, the creases that naturally occur when you wear linen should be embraced. Just as a favourite pair of shoes will mould to your feet, your linen will mould to you as you wear it. You can't totally stop those creases – they will pop up one way or another somewhere.

If you can't stand the faff or the inevitable creasing from a 100% linen garment, look for pieces with a linen mix that may be less prone to creasing. Linen/Viscose mix fabrics are a good option as they are still breathable and sustainable.

Always remember that your clothes are an investment and like all great investments, you need to look after them to keep them performing at their best.

Before I buy anything, I usually look at the garment care label to see what it is made of and whether it is washable. I rarely buy things that can't be washed due to the hassle and expense of taking things to a dry cleaner for chemical cleaning. However, the most expensive items in the wardrobe are most likely to be 'Dry Clean Only' garments, which isn't too much of a problem if they are something that you don't wear very often.

When it comes to washing, most items do not need to be washed after every time you wear them (obviously, underwear, workout gear and swimwear excluded). Consider how often you wash your clothes, given that every wash will start to erode the fabrics and possibly the colours, too.

As a guide, the following number of wears before washing is recommended.

- T-shirts and tops: one or two

- Dresses: two to three

- Pajamas: three to four

- Sweatshirts and jumpers: five to six

- Skirts: five to seven

- Jeans: six to ten

Using the "sniff test" to see if your garment smells sweaty and your common sense is a good way forward.

Before washing, always check the label of the garment first. Most things can be washed in a machine on a 30-degree cycle with a medium spin. High spins might get the water out to help your garment dry more quickly; however, the force of the spin risks stretching your garment out of shape, so whilst not an issue for tough fabrics like denim, this may be damaging for gentler fabrics or those featuring embellishments. In this case, use a zipped mesh laundry bag, which you can buy from the laundry aisle of most supermarkets or place your garment inside a pillowcase and then into your washing machine.

Separate your laundry pile into whites, darks and colours, as different colours require different detergents.

Always wash your garments inside out to preserve colours and help reduce fading. This also protects any embellishments on the garment, like stitching, beading, or printed designs.

Laundry Icons

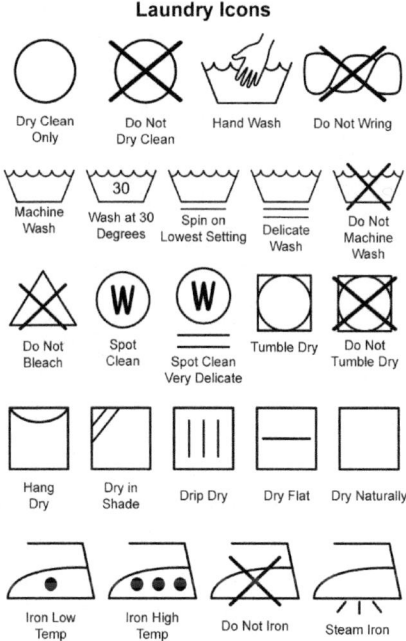

This handy guide to the symbols on laundry labels will help you know what to do when washing, drying or ironing your clothing. Remember, every time you wash your clothes or use a tumble dryer, slight elements of the fabrics will be removed. It's a bit like hair every time you brush your hair, some of it will fall out and be left on the brush, so the more you brush, the more you lose.

Depending on your garment, the detergent you use is another key consideration. Most laundry detergents are classified as 'Bio', meaning they contain biological cleaning agents that may be bleach-based, or 'non-bio', meaning they don't. Different types of detergent, such as powder, liquids or pods, add complications.

Powder detergents can contain aggressive bleaching agents and are not recommended for delicate fabrics. However, powders will often give a better whitewash result.

Non-bio-liquid detergents usually do not contain bleaching agents. They can be used directly on a stain for spot cleaning before washing, and they're great for handwashing as they dissolve quickly. I also find them a great option used neat for cleaning up white trainers.

You can choose liquid in a pod or the pouring kind. Check the back of the pod packaging to see the lowest temperature wash the pod is designed to dissolve at; otherwise, you may find residue attached to your clothes when the wash cycle has finished.

New eco egg options or wash sheets can be used if environmental issues are really important to you.

Bio detergent is a good option for helping to keep your whites bright...rather than old socks grey.

For most other things, non-bio is an option, or you can use a coloured wash liquid, which specifically helps your garments retain their colours.

White vinegar is excellent for laundry and is cheap to purchase. Adding white vinegar to your wash will help keep denim supple, preserve the vibrancy of coloured garments, combat B.O. smells and keep your whites a little whiter.

Use detergents containing stain remover sparingly and only when garments have nasty, stubborn stains that need removing after spot cleaning. Overusing stain removers will fade your clothes as they are harsher than regular detergents due to their chemical composition.

Some fabrics – especially Viscose can give the impression that they have shrunk in the wash as the fibres contract, but they will spring back to shape if you iron or steam them. Drying garments on a washing line or indoors after gently reshaping is always a favourable option over a tumble dryer, as it helps combat shrinkage or fabric degradation. Be careful that your washing is not drying in full sun, as this can cause fading to any material.

Always double-check the label first to see whether your knitwear can be washed. Some knitwear can only be dry cleaned, and if it is a really thick knit, it may be a handwash-only garment, needing intensive care for it to keep its shape.

Knitwear should always be washed separately from other garments using a detergent specifically designed for the purpose, like Woolite. This helps to protect the fibres of your knitwear and keep them fluffy, whereas detergents can stick to the fibres and be hard to wash out.

You should dry your knitwear flat, which is easier said than done if you live in an apartment or have minimal space. The best approach is to gently squeeze out the excess water after washing (without twisting or wringing), then lay your knit flat onto a large towel before rolling it up inside the towel to create a giant knitwear sausage roll. This way, the towel absorbs the excess water so that when you unroll it later, the weight has been taken out of your knit, helping to retain its shape as it dries.

Looking after knitwear is easier if you always wear a base layer of clothing beneath it. This means you do not have to wash the knitwear as often, as your base layer will absorb any body odours or sweat and is easier to wash and dry frequently.

Sometimes, little bobbles can appear on your knitwear. This could be after washing or sometimes it is just where the fabrics in the knit rub against something like a handbag or your arm rubbing against your side. These bobbles can easily be removed using an inexpensive cashmere comb. Some people use battery-operated "bobble machines" too. The key thing to remember when de-bobbling is to be careful, depending on the thickness of the threads in the knit. If it is a super fine knit, I would not recommend using anything except your fingers to pinch and gently remove bobbles. Mid-weight and thicker knits will be fine. Lay your knitwear flat and comb it with the cashmere comb in a slow, deliberate, continuous movement from top to bottom. This will scrape off the bobbles and restore your knitwear to smooth condition.

If your garment needs ironing, ensure it is turned inside out and always iron on the reverse side following instructions on the garment care label. This helps prevent bobbling, fading or sheen and protects any prints, detailing or buttons. Sometimes steaming is a better option.

Homework

Ensure you have a range of laundry detergents to use appropriately for washing different garments.

Buy a laundry net bag for washing bras, delicate or embellished items.

Always check the labels on your garments before washing.

Invest in a cashmere comb or de-bobbling machine to keep your knitwear in good shape.

LOOK GOOD AND FEEL FANTASTIC

Chapter 11

Do You Really Need That?

"I'm just trying to change the world,
one sequin at a time."

Lady Gaga

After detoxing your wardrobe and feeling good about the pieces you have, it's easy to fall into the trap of buying too many clothes once again. You will probably have discovered some gaps in your collection or may need to replace key pieces that have been subject to wear and tear. Temptation can slowly lead you back to having lots of items bulking out your wardrobe again if you are not careful.

Just like a road safety campaign, it is important to stop and think before you hit the shops or go online shopping and consider your cost per wear. Yes, it's maths — but it's not that bad. You simply divide the item's price by the number of times you wear it. For example, if you buy a piece of clothing costing £100 and wear it 100 times, then that piece of clothing has reduced its cost per wear to £0 and if you wear it more than 100 times you are in negative number territory (woohoo you win). However, if you purchase something for £35 as a 'bargain' in a sale and never wear it, then that item has still cost you £35 (boo, you lose)! You should buy items you love in colours that suit you, your body shape and your style personality to coordinate with other pieces in your wardrobe that you want to wear all the time to save money by buying less in the long term.

Two-in-one garments are a good purchase as they can give you at least two different looks from one item, saving you space in your wardrobe. This is a good option when packing for travelling and also good value for money, as they usually cost less than the price of two separate garments. Look for items that are reversible or can be worn with different necklines or different prints on the front and back.

There will be items of clothing that you will need to regularly replace as they are high-usage pieces, but the cost-per-wear strategy helps you understand that initially investing a little more on quality pieces that are built to last and are classics will ultimately save you money compared to cheaper alternatives that may be lesser quality or more trend-based.

I'm not saying don't embrace a fashion trend, if that trend suits you and your style personality and it's a piece you will wear repeatedly, bringing your cost per wear down to £0, then absolutely go for it. However, if you have doubts about how often you will wear the item, I recommend you steer clear.

I went to a Chanel exhibition at the V&A Museum in London. Gabrielle Chanel (also known as Coco Chanel) was a remarkable French haute couture fashion designer. It was interesting to learn more about her story, from humble beginnings designing hats to becoming the style icon she was, dressing so many famous people, including royalty. What I hadn't appreciated before going to this exhibition was her legacy.

Before the exhibition, I was a little sceptical about designer clothing being more a case of overpaying for a name or brand than the quality of the clothing, but boy, was I wrong in the case of Chanel! Seeing the garments up close made it clear that it's much more than this. The detailing in the garments was just insane – the amount of stitching of embellishments such as beading or sequins, which were hand-sewn, was just mind-blowing. The structure of pieces behind the designs was scientific, such as adding weights in the hemlines of jackets to help them hang beautifully when worn. Chanel was clearly a designer ahead of her time and so many items of quality clothing today feature aspects of her original designs that we don't realise.

The old adage "you get what you pay for" is true when choosing clothing. This is harder to ascertain when shopping online as you rely on photographs that can sometimes be manipulated or don't always represent the actual quality or colour of the garment due to the effects of studio lighting.

Being able to see, touch, and feel a piece of clothing before you buy it will usually give you some good clues to the quality and construction of the piece, especially when you look at the seams on the inside where the stitching should be neat and straight on a quality piece. Also, looking at how the garments are displayed in the shop is another clue. Are the garments treated like they are treasured, or are they treated like trash? Is the store tidy and clean, and are garments neatly displayed, or are garments falling off hangers, on the floor, or messily piled up on tables? All of it builds a picture behind the brand for you to consider whether it is a brand you trust.

If you can't resist a bargain and end up with pieces in your wardrobe with the tags on unworn, then I recommend steering clear of the sales and unsubscribing from the email lists of clothing retailers so that you can avoid temptation when that email pings into your inbox with their latest "must-have, buy it now" piece.

Avoid online clothes shopping late at night – I think everyone at some time has put items into their basket and checked out only to find when they arrive they are not quite right – maybe they were cheap, and you actually can't be bothered to go through the whole shenanigans of returning items via the post...so you don't! Sometimes, you may have been scammed by a fast fashion importer posing as another business in a different county "closing down". In this case, the retailer or scammer "wins" as they have taken your cash and sold you an item (regardless of whether you need it or not) and you lose as you have an item that you don't want but may cost you money to return and is now clogging up your wardrobe space.

It's important to consider how often you will wear a particular piece of clothing, where it comes from, and how it is made. Look at the garment's seams to see how well it has been constructed. The stitching lines should be straight rather than wiggly, with buttons, zips, or fasteners having robust stitching and neatly finished buttonholes. If you spot loose threads or unfinished areas, this is a warning sign of a mass-produced item with poor quality control, meaning your garment may not last very long before it has some malfunction that needs attention.

Brand awareness is something else to consider. Do you know the credentials of the brand that you are buying? Do they shout about their eco-policies or ethics of supporting the businesses behind the brand that may produce the fabrics and/or garments? Where are the garments made? What are they made from? What happens in the production process? Whilst it may state a country of origin on the fabric label inside the garment, this is not always the case for the whole garment, which may involve several countries in the construction of the piece.

Some brands are of lower quality, pile it high and sell it cheap, often following fads or short-lived trends, earning them the name "Fast Fashion". Unsold items from the stock of these brands can commonly be sent to landfill sites having never been worn. If you think about that for a minute, imagine the whole growing/production process for fabric, then the printing, design and cutting, stitching, packaging, shipping (often from overseas) and the transport to the shop or online warehouse – all that time, money, water, chemicals, fuel and pollution only to be disposed of having never been worn. It really is quite shocking.

A quality brand will always tell you what its policies are. They usually shout about their eco credentials and how they reduce their impact on the planet regarding how their garments are produced. Often (but not always), they will use recycled materials in some of their garments and look for ways to reduce the overuse of water or chemicals in the production process. If you are not sure about the stance of the brands that you like, I recommend going to their company websites and doing a search – those that are ethical will be shouting about it from the rooftops, whereas those that are less concerned will be a bit sketchy about what they do or don't say anything at all on the matter.

For a fabric to earn the term "eco-friendly," it has to meet specific criteria, such as having no or minimal amounts of toxic chemicals, such as synthetic dyes and bleach. New developments are happening constantly.

The Presenter, Stacey Dooley, once did one of her reporting TV programmes investigating the truth behind cotton growing and sustainability in fashion. It was fascinating in a relaxed, easy-to-watch reporting style and worth watching if you like documentaries. This programme highlighted the incomprehensible amounts of water needed to grow cotton and how cotton is viewed as an eco-fabric. However, cultivating the cotton for the fabric is anything but.

Many garments are being created from former fabrics such as recycled polyester/nylon or recycled natural fabrics like cotton. Recycled cotton is more eco-friendly than "pure" cotton as it uses less water in the production process than it takes to grow the cotton plant from scratch.

Preventing pollution from the fashion industry has filtered out further to the companies who make laundry products, as we have suddenly realised that our wastewater goes somewhere – often to the sea. Washing machine wastewater will contain tiny fabric particles that have come away in the washing process and are too small to be picked up by wastewater filtration systems. One solution to this problem has been the development of a "Guppy Bag", a fine mesh bag you put your garments into before putting them into a washing machine. Not only does this type of wash bag protect your garments in the washing process, but it also helps to contain those tiny fibres within the bag, which can be binned after washing rather than going through the wastewater filtration process and off into the sea.

Homework

Consider 2-in-1 garments that can be worn more than one way — remember, these may already be features of your wardrobe, but you may not have previously considered wearing them differently.

Think about the ethics and eco credentials of the brands you usually buy. If you don't know, visit their company websites and find out. You may be cheering at how good they are or reconsider whether you continue to spend your hard-earned cash with those companies if not.

Stop and think before making your next clothing purchase, especially if you shop online late at night.

Unsubscribe from retailer email newsletters to avoid the temptation of overspending.

Chapter 12

Building A Capsule Wardrobe

"I want everyone to wear what
they want and mix it in their own way..."
Karl Lagerfeld

The next part of your style journey is to examine how you combine individual pieces of clothing to create outfits that can be worn as part of a capsule wardrobe.

A capsule wardrobe is a collection of garments that work well together and can be mixed and matched to create multiple outfits. Having a capsule wardrobe will make your life so much easier. When you open those wardrobe doors and select your clothes, you don't have to put too much thought into it, as everything "goes." All the pieces work together, and you will have fewer pieces in your wardrobe, saving you money in the longer term.

Having fewer pieces in your wardrobe that work hard for you may allow you to invest in more costly items you wouldn't usually have had the cash to buy. A particular Designer coat in a classic cut that will never go out of style may be something that is now within reach, and you don't have to always buy pieces brand new. Dress Agencies and re-sale sites such as Vinted are great for finding 'new to you' designer pieces. Oxfam has a dedicated designer clothes second-hand shop online too.

Once you have the basis of your capsule wardrobe, you will find it much easier when clothes shopping. It will be easy to introduce a new trend by style or colour (if that is something you want to do) or a new top, shirt, accessory or piece of jewellery to complete your outfits. I love scouting the charity shops for interesting and unique pieces of jewellery, which are a low-cost way to update an outfit.

For the best effect for a piece to work in your capsule wardrobe, you need to consider how you can wear that piece in three different ways. For example, jeans could be worn super casual with a sweatshirt, dressed up for coffee with friends with a top and jacket, or strappy heels and a sparkly top with statement jewellery for a night out.

Dresses are not just dresses when considering how to wear them three ways. For example, a buttoned-up shirt dress can be worn unbuttoned over a strappy top and jeans for a "shacket" (shirt worn as a jacket) effect. Wear a chunky knit over your dress and add boots for a dressed-down feel. Or you could wear your dress...as a dress.

When you consider how accessories, such as a scarf, jewellery, bags, shoes, etc., can change the look of your garment, then those three ways of wearing that piece will increase even further.

Another key consideration is layering pieces. These are pieces that can be worn on top of one another to create an overall outfit. It's not about deliberately wearing everything you've got in one go like Joey in 'that' episode of Friends, but more about how those pieces complement each other and add to the overall effect of the outfit. It's about styling your clothes rather than just wearing them and giving you the flexibility to adapt to your environment, which is particularly important if you are going through menopause or at the perimenopause stage and dealing with hot flushes and a changing body shape as part of your new "norm".

For menopausal dressing, a key consideration has to be the type of fabrics your clothes are made of. To combat those hot flushes, you need to look for breathable fabrics. Natural fabrics like viscose or cotton will become your best friend, along with pieces you can quickly and easily remove when you are hot before replacing easily once the flush has passed. This may be a key consideration as part of your wardrobe if you work in front of clients or in a professional environment.

Some pieces should form the basis of every wardrobe, irrespective of your body shape or style – these are your go-to pieces that will form the building blocks of outfits and your base layers that will see you through all seasons.

Every capsule wardrobe needs a pair of jeans, a smarter pair of trousers, short-sleeve and long-sleeve base layer tops, a casual and a smarter knit, a casual and a smarter jacket, a coat and some tops that can be dressed up and down to suit. How many pieces are up to you and your style personality. Similarly, dresses and/or skirts may form part of your capsule collection if these are something that you enjoy wearing regularly, but if you are "not a dress person", then it's more important to go for the pieces that you will wear and that will work for the lifestyle that you live.

If you work in a professional environment, you can separate your wardrobe into two capsule collections: one that contains all the options for your working wardrobe and the other with all the pieces for life outside of work. However, you may find that some of your tops are multitaskers and work for both – in which case, hang these in the middle.

The art of layering your clothing starts from the base foundations and works outwards. A base layer may be a short-sleeve plain T-shirt or vest top; moving to the next layer, a shirt, jumper or tank top, a jacket and an outer coat and a woolly scarf in winter; however, in summer, it may be a vest top beneath an open shirt for some protection from the sun with a lightweight scarf (that you can also use as a sarong).

When pulling your outfits together, three is still a magic number – you have the rule of thirds for your body shape, pieces in your wardrobe that can be worn three ways and now you need to consider no more than three different colours for the best effect when you build your outfit. Sticking to no more than three colours means that your eye will automatically "match" the colours to give balance to your outfit. If you go for more colours than three, the effect can overwhelm the eye and look "wrong". The colours of nature are all about symmetry and complementary colours, which also apply when outfit building if you want to get your overall look right.

There is even more science behind the colours you choose and what they portray, which we will discuss in another chapter. However, looking at a colour wheel is a great place to start when considering which colours go together.

Colour Wheel

The colours that sit next to each other on the colour wheel will work together for your outfit and the colours opposite each other will also work well. You can mix colours equal distances apart on the colour wheel too, aiming for no more than three colours in your outfit. The only exception is if you wear a print featuring many colours, in which case, wear the print and pick out one of the tones from the print to balance your look.

Another option is to look at tonal dressing rather than matching complementary colours. Here, you can use various tones of the same colour when building your outfit, for example, blue jeans with a pale blue top and a bright blue jacket over.

Colour blocking is when you build your outfit in the same colour from head to toe. This is a handy trick if you are petite, as it gives the illusion of height, as your silhouette is elongated and not broken up by other colours.

You may have heard of the phrase "sandwiching" (which isn't munching your lunch and spilling the filling on your top). Sandwiching is building an outfit based on two colourways; the top of your outfit (or your hair) and your footwear will be the same colour, but what you wear in the middle will be a different but complementary colour, like looking at the filling between the bread of the sandwich.

Homework

Review your key pieces that form the basis of the foundations of your capsule wardrobe.

Organise the pieces in your wardrobe by colour if helpful.

Consider how you can wear each piece in your wardrobe in three different ways as part of your capsule collection. If you can't wear it three ways, it may be time to get rid of it or store it separately.

Chapter 13
She Wears It Well

"Learn the rules like a pro, so you can break them like an artist."
Pablo Picasso

The art of dressing well is not just about getting the proper fit of clothes to suit your body shape but also how you bring your outfits together. Styling an outfit with accessories, footwear, layering pieces and your colour choices contribute to the overall effect. Styling the garments that make up your outfit will give it a very different look and feel rather than just wearing your clothes.

If you have been a savvy shopper, you will have already bought pieces that can be worn in more than one way – perhaps an item is reversible or can be worn backwards to give a different look.

It is definitely worth looking creatively at your clothing and really thinking outside of the box. You may have pieces in your wardrobe that you like which have slightly outdated features. There may be an alternative way to wear the item that brings new life to it. For instance, a shirt with a wide collar may look a little dated, but if you tuck the wide collar inside the shirt and under your bra strap, it will stay in place and give a v-neckline to the shirt instead, which may suit your body shape better.

I am a huge advocate of looking at a garment to see if it can be worn upside down. Quite often, knitwear is excellent for this, especially if it is a long-bodied piece that finishes around the hip or thigh area, which may not be a flattering length for your body shape. Simply wearing the piece upside down so that the waist of the garment is at your neckline and the neck of the garment is at your waist will give a boxier waist-length finish, with any excess material falling like a cowl neckline or scarf effect.

Maxi-length skirts – especially those with elasticated waistbands and a straight front waist can sometimes be worn pulled up over your boobs as a strapless dress – adding a belt to give definition to your waist too.

Consider wearing a shirt open "jacket style" over a plain T-shirt or top. If the shirt is too long, tie a knot in each end to shorten the length, or you can tie the two ends together behind your back to give it a bolero effect.

The type of footwear you choose can also change the look of your outfit. A dress for a smart/casual brunch may feature kitten-heeled or flat shoes. However, that dress may be paired with a strappy heel for a more elevated party look. If you shop and have coffee with friends, wear trainers with the dress for a more relaxed look. All will give a slightly different feel.

Your choice of footwear is just as important as your other accessories. Some clothing items require particular pieces of footwear for the best effect. For example, bootcut jeans are best worn over boots, with trainers or strappy heels, whereas a wide-leg jean will look good when worn with platform trainers, a funky patterned low heel or a flat shoe.

Choosing shoes in the right shape or colour to complement your outfit and style personality will help you with your overall look, especially if you add jewellery and a belt, a scarf or a hat to complete your outfit to give you different looks and styles.

Depending on the outfit and occasion, you can make a statement by choosing big, bold-coloured jewellery and accessories or opt for a more minimalist look by choosing simple silver or gold jewellery. This is where you can really incorporate the characteristics of your style personality when building your outfits.

Also a general rule of thumb, it's best to keep metallics to similar shades. If you wear a top with silver metallic threads or sequins, then follow that through with silver-coloured metals in your jewellery. Similarly, a top or dress with gold sequins, threads or chain detailing will work best paired with gold shoes and gold-coloured jewellery. Having said that, rules are made to be broken. There is no problem in wearing mixed metals together, provided your clothing doesn't contain any metallics at all (or it contains both colours of the same metallics in your jewellery).

Different styles of necklace work better for different-shaped necklines of garments and getting this right will help balance the look of your outfit.

Wear a longer necklace for a boat neckline. Look for necklaces that finish at the ribs or dangle down towards your belly button.

A Scoop neckline works well with statement jewellery that sits between your neck and the scoop. Alternatively, a dainty chain with a pendant that finishes just below your bra strap can look good too.

For a crew neckline, opt for necklaces that sit just below the hem edge of the neckline on the garment. Statement pieces will also work well here.

V Necklines suit pieces that fall into the V shape. Layered necklaces work for this, as do delicate necklaces with pendants, but make sure they do not fall below the deepest part of the V of your top.

Shorter-length necklaces work well with collared shirts. Again, opt for pieces that sit closer to your skin and are not "lost" below the shirt's buttons.

Opt for a chunky chain necklace with a statement-size pendant attached for a sweetheart neckline. Again, the length of the necklace should be higher than the deepest part of the neckline of your top for the best effect.

A choker necklace will look stunning on a strapless or off-the-shoulder top (remember Princess Diana in her pearl choker necklace with a black off-the-shoulder dress that caused a stir?). If you can't bear things that are fitted at the neck, go for a statement necklace that sits just over your top instead.

For a cowl neckline, you can go long or short. Again, ensure that anything short sits inside the neckline and fills the gap between your neck and the cowl. A longer-length necklace should aim to finish below the drapes of the cowl neck over your top.

As with necklaces, the type of bag you choose to accompany your outfit will most likely be different depending on the occasion; for example, a night out may only need a small phone carrier-size bag or clutch bag, the smart/casual brunch may feature a cross-body bag, or your choice when going shopping and for coffee with friends is probably a tote bag that can accommodate all your purchases.

Colour choices for your bag can come down to your style personality. If you are an extrovert, you may have a wardrobe full of bags in every shade of the rainbow, choosing a brightly coloured distinctive bag for each outfit. Alternatively, you may be a person who can't stand the faff of swapping everything between bags, opting for neutral shades of bags from high-end brands or metallic shades that you can pair with many outfits, taking up less space in your wardrobe.

Homework

Take a creative look at the garments in your wardrobe and think outside the box, to see how you can wear pieces differently when styling.

Can you wear it upside down?

I bet most of the bags in your wardrobe are never used! Consider your bag collection and your style personality. If you have bags in every colour you never use and are more of a classic style personality, it may be time to declutter those bags and keep a small selection of neutral colours/shapes and metallics that will work with your outfits and give you some space back.

Consider your necklace collection against the necklines of the tops and dresses in your wardrobe. If you need a longer necklace to suit the neckline, why not join two necklaces together at the clasp?

LOOK GOOD AND FEEL FANTASTIC

Chapter 14

Myths and Legends

"Life is a sea of vibrant colour. Jump in."

A.D. Posey

When it comes to styling outfits, there are a few myths and legends that we need to dispel.

"I can't wear red."

This is rubbish! Everyone can wear red – there are over 100 shades of red to choose from and a shade of red for everyone if you look for it. Red is a bold colour choice and needs confidence to carry it off in volume. However, if confidence is not your strongest point, you can introduce red to your outfit through accessories. A piece of red jewellery against a neutral outfit will add impact or go for a scarf that contains red in the pattern.

Purple or blue-based reds will work best for a winter or summer colour palette, whereas a more orangey or bright poppy/tomato red will work well for a spring colour palette. A rusty red is perfect for an autumnal colour palette – you just need to find the right shade that works for you and wear the quantity of red that feels right for you.

"I can't wear black."

Everyone can wear black...even when they can't wear black! That may sound confusing, but if your colour palette shies away from black, you can still wear it – just not near your face. Wear black below the waist in jeans/trousers/skirts or as part of an outfit with a neutral or brighter-coloured top that works for you.

If you have a black dress, choose a neckline that exposes as much skin as possible to soften the look, or wear a scarf by your face in a colour or pattern that suits you and complements the black. If you don't want to wear black clothes, go for black accessories – a black bag, shoes or jewellery.

"I can't wear white."

A bit like red – there are at least 50 shades of white and again, it is a case of finding the right shade that works for you. If your colour palette is warm, look for shades of ecru or warm whites verging on cream. If your colour palette is cool, ice white will really pop against your complexion. A plain white shirt (or ecru shirt) is a wardrobe staple that looks great dressed down paired with a simple pair of blue jeans or dressed up as part of a smarter look.

"If you wear black and blue you look like a bruise!"

Rubbish! Black and blue are the perfect colours to wear together, provided you think carefully about the shades. Generally speaking, a darker/midnight blue works fab with a true black, whereas a paler shade of blue looks great with a more charcoal shade of black that is not quite so dense. Just like red and white, there are multiple shades and it's a case of finding the right one for you. The texture of the fabric will play a huge part as a heavier textured piece will dissolve the "blackness" when your eye looks at the piece, as the light will be reflected over the textures. In contrast, a plainer, smoother fabric with less texture absorbs more of the "blackness" when your eye looks at it, making the black appear more intense. So don't rule out wearing black with blue and play around with mixing different fabric textures when you put your outfit together. If you are not confident mixing a black garment with a blue one, look for a print that combines both of these colours in a garment or a scarf. Black and blue funky animal prints can be a fun way to wear these colours together.

"Double denim doesn't work."

This is another myth! Just like ensuring you get the right shades of colours, it is a case of matching the right shades of denim. You need to go for shades that are as identical as possible for a colour block look or choose shades that complement each other without looking like they clash. Your choice of accessories can help bridge the gap between shades of denim; it is just a case of playing around to see what works and what doesn't. Double denim is a very popular look in French fashion, where you can often buy pieces crafted from complementary shades of denim so that you don't have the hassle of working out which pieces to match as it's already been done for you. A patterned scarf can bridge the gap by blending the shades of different denim, especially when worn as a belt.

"You can't mix prints in your outfit."

At the risk of sounding like a pantomime audience, "Oh yes, you can!"

Mixing prints is an excellent way of building an outfit with a presence. The trick when mixing prints is to choose prints with similar colours and sizes in the print. A small geometric print will work great with a small dotty or abstract print, provided that both prints have some colours in common and the same applies to larger prints. Just keep the pattern size in each piece similar and voila! The exception to this rule is leopard prints where larger and smaller leopard prints will complement each other beautifully in your overall outfit.

"Stripes will make you look bigger than you are."

This one is partly true and partly false. You may have been told that horizontal stripes worn on the body will make you look larger as the eye is drawn to the ends of the stripes. However, if the stripey item is a Breton T-shirt, for example, wearing it beneath a jacket or blazer will mean that only the front of the stripe is on show, so it will not make you look wider than you are, as the stripes finish in the middle of your body.

You also need to consider how broad the stripes are. A finer stripe will deceive the eye into thinking that the stripes merge and will be fine. Broader stripes, especially those in bold or striking colours, can work well if you have an hourglass figure, as they positively accentuate the waistline.

Vertical stripes on a garment can make you appear taller. However, depending on which colour of the stripe is at the outline of your silhouette, it may make you appear a little wider than you are if they are very bold stripes. As with horizontal stripes, you will be ok if it is a fine stripe in similar colours.

If you want to give the impression of a longer, slimmer leg, look for a garment featuring piping or a stripe along the outer seam. This blends your silhouette with the background and deceives the eye to focus on the width of the largest fabric patch. The key here is to ensure that the piping or striped seam sits in the right place on you to create this optical illusion, which you will only discover by trying on the garment and looking at yourself in a mirror.

"Animal prints are tacky."

No, no, no, no, no! It is quite the contrary! Leopard print is, in fact, officially a "neutral" as it goes with everything! The trick with wearing an animal print is to match the tones behind the print with the other pieces in your outfit. If it's a black and tan animal print, stick to black or tan pieces in your outfit or accessories. If it is a black and darker brown animal print, stick to black and darker brown shades when building your outfit.

Just like red, if you are not confident enough to wear the print in your garments, start by wearing the print in your accessories. Pair leopard-print shoes with your jeans or wear a leopard-print scarf over a plain shirt. You can even start with a leopard-print bracelet and slowly build up until you have confidence.

"Never mix gold and silver."

Poppycock! Mixing and matching your gold and silver jewellery together is totally acceptable! When it comes to clothing, metallics certainly have their day for a bit of retro style, festive or evening dressing! The trick to wearing silver and gold together (or any other metallic, for that matter) is finding the shades that work well. A paler champagne version of gold will work well paired with silver as they are similar shades; equally, a more pewter-based metallic works well with silver as they are both shades of grey. Mixing shades of the same metallics works well.

You will get a more balanced look by keeping to the same type of metallic across all your outfit accessories. For instance, a belt with a silver buckle will look better worn with silver-coloured jewellery or trainers with silver eyelets, but if mixing things up is your own style personality, go for it. Rules are made to be broken after all!

Homework

When it comes to colours, nothing is off limits – you need to find the right shade that works for you, so experiment.

Hold colours against your face and look in the mirror to determine what does and does not suit or take a selfie instead. When you look back at the photo, you will instantly feel if that is the right shade or colour for you, depending on whether it brightens or dulls your complexion.

Play around with pairing textures and prints to discover new outfits from your wardrobe. You may be pleasantly surprised at how many new outfit combinations you can make from pieces you already own and have never considered putting together.

Chapter 15

Style File

"Style is wearing an evening dress to McDonalds"
John Galliano

By now you may be realising that a pattern is starting to emerge. You are probably drawn to specific colours, which might be your favourite colour. Still, you may not have noticed how much that colour influences your wardrobe. Some people find that their wardrobe is pretty much all the same colour (especially my husband – he always gravitates towards blue), just differing shades or tones. This is not a problem. This is a good thing as it means that the pieces in your wardrobe will automatically work together. You have already begun building a capsule wardrobe, perhaps without realising that you were doing it.

If you haven't already, look at each of those pieces in the wardrobe and consider if they "fit" the Style Personality you identified in Chapter 2. If you find it hard to declutter and need a few goes to get rid of things gradually, then taking another look specifically with your style personality in mind can help narrow things down. If you are a classic personality that likes clean lines and subtle detailing, it may be time to say goodbye to that sequin jacket that would look perfectly at home on 'Strictly Come Dancing.'

Thinking again about your lifestyle, you need to have clothes ready in your wardrobe that suit your daily life and style personality.

Keeping a style file can be a good source of inspiration and is easy to do on your mobile phone. If you are anything like me, you probably have signed up to receive various retailer newsletters along the way or follow pages on Facebook or Instagram.

I recommend that you create a separate album for your phone photos. When you see something you like and think would work for you, take a photo/screenshot and save it to your folder to build up a style file for inspiration when styling your outfits.

You may like the clothes a particular celebrity wears, or it may be an advert you have seen. Add the pictures to your file to consider how to adapt that look to work for you. I am not suggesting that you replicate precisely how that person is wearing their outfit, but more so that you take inspiration from it to see how elements can work for you. After all, everyone is different, and your body shape may be totally different to the person in the image.

Having a style file of inspiration can help you identify things you may be missing when outfit building or find pieces you may want to add to your capsule wardrobe if you like to follow garment and/or colour trends.

Looking back at the images, you will most likely be drawn to specific themes.

Maybe Kate Moss's rock chick style is your thing, and your wardrobe features skinny jeans, black leather jackets, sleek tailoring, studded items or metal zips and biker boots.

Perhaps a French style is more your thing: short boxy Chanel-style jackets, Breton-striped T-shirts, cigarette-cut trousers, asymmetric detailing and a little *je ne sais quoi.*

You may travel frequently for holiday or work purposes and your wardrobe may hold more layering pieces in neutral colours and comfortable fabrics that travel well without creasing.

You may work in a professional office environment where suits and more tailored items are the order of the day. Bright-coloured tops may be your go-to, especially if you have a lot of online calls or presentation meetings.

You may be a mum to younger children, where practicality is the name of the game. You may live in your trainers with jeans and long-sleeved T-shirts that you can layer up and adapt to whatever you have planned (or unplanned) for your day. Jumpers, easy-to-wear jackets, warm outdoor coats for school runs and boots that can have a smart or casual look will most probably feature.

You may find yourself drawn to vintage looks or have many retro-style pieces in your wardrobe. Some people enjoy replicating a 1950s style with a modern twist regarding patterns or dress shapes.

You may be sporty, and leisurewear is a key look for you. Often, the teenage years gravitate towards this look, but it's not exclusive to any age range. Baggy jeans, oversized jumpers/sweatshirts, leggings and Ugg boot-style footwear or trainers may be the look you like best, or they may fit your lifestyle now.

As you read through, elements from different styles may resonate with you and are the kind of look you like and wear occasionally. This is precisely the point about everyone being different and demonstrates how a style file can help you mix and match things from various sources into an outfit that works for you.

When you piece together an outfit combination that you really like, feels great and gives you confidence, take a photograph of yourself in the mirror and add that to your style file to have a visual record to remind you. This helps prevent you from having things in the back of the wardrobe that get forgotten about and ensures you are getting your cost per wear from your investment in your clothing collection. It's also a handy quick reference guide if you have one of those "I don't know what to wear for..." moments.

Homework

Set up a photo album on your phone to create your style file.

When you see images of items or outfits you like, take a photograph or screenshot and add it to your style file.

When you wear an outfit that looks good and makes you feel good, take a selfie and add it to your style file as a reminder for another day when you may need some outfit inspiration.

Chapter 16

What You See is Not Necessarily What You Get

"There is only going to be one Kate Moss.

Kate is an icon."

Naomi Campbell

Social media is such a big part of everyone's life these days. With online shopping increasing, AI is becoming more widely used to create images and texts.

Online shopping can be tricky for several reasons. I am sure I am not the only one who has ever ordered something online, only to be disappointed when it arrives because it is smaller than it looks or a different colour from how it was portrayed on screen. So, you have to treat the images you see online as only a guide.

Some retailers have worked hard to portray garments' colours accurately in online shop images. In contrast, others have done less – especially those with a higher volume of garments and a quicker turnover of new styles dropping frequently.

Clever camera angles can distort an image and the lighting when the photograph is taken will affect how the colour appears on screen. This is especially true if the picture is taken in a studio against a white background, where it may seem more washed out than it really is.

Remember that the device you are viewing the images on will also distort the colours in the image. If you load an image on your phone and a computer or laptop, you will likely find that the colours in that same image look different on each device. This is down to the settings on the device and how it wants to portray the colour to you.

Most images will have been photoshopped or airbrushed to some degree, too. This is very important as it is very easy to get drawn into making comparisons of yourself with a model who appears to have perfect skin, longer legs, a slimmer body, etc. The reality may be that the model is spotty, but the imperfections have been airbrushed. They may not be the long, thin person you see, as the image may have been edited.

I went to a fantastic Naomi Campbell exhibition at the V&A Museum in London, showcasing her story from being discovered, the designers she has worked with and displayed her most iconic fashion pieces that she had worn in various catwalk shows and photo shoots. I came away quite unexpectedly and pleasantly surprised by that exhibition.

The image sold to us of Naomi Campbell is a 6ft, size 0 model. However, the displayed outfits confirmed that this is pleasingly not the case!

I think Naomi is 5ft 10", a little shorter than portrayed. Also, the pieces on display looked more like a size 6 to an 8 at different points in her career, so not the "stick insect" size 0 portrayed in the media at all!

The thing that sets Naomi Campbell apart is her very long legs – her muscle structure is so well defined and toned from a background of dance, which is her "secret weapon" and why she appears to be taller than she really is in the images that are portrayed on screen...along with those infamous platform shoes worn in the Vivienne Westwood show when she famously fell over!

It's an important lesson about taking what the media sells to you with a pinch of salt. It's a fantastic exhibition, so if you ever see it advertised, please go!

I appreciate that not everyone wants to look like a supermodel or have the body of a supermodel. Still, you can take inspiration for your style personality from the images you see in the media. Certain celebrities consistently ooze their style in bucketloads, sometimes in the characters played on screen or in their private lives.

We can't help but be bombarded with images on TV, bus shelters, magazines, newspapers, social media, and cinema, to name just a few, so you can take a mental note of what you like and aim to replicate that from your own wardrobe to steal their style.

If you like a tailored classic look, turn to Victoria Beckham for inspiration. Alternatively, Jennifer

Aniston's clothing choices may tick your boxes if you prefer a neutral, smart, casual LA look.

If you have a dramatic style personality and love art, you may be inspired by Dame Prue Leith, who is always in bright colours with large, dramatic, eye-catching necklaces when appearing on TV.

Or does the distinctive "London" rock chic Kate Moss style or that of Mary Portas resonate with you?

Whatever your style personality is, you will find inspiration from various people and places that you can tweak and build into the outfits you enjoy wearing. The main thing is that when you know what suits you and your body shape, experiment a little and play around mixing old and new pieces maybe with a touch of vintage too so that you build a wardrobe of pieces that you will wear time and time again, that suit you and give you confidence when you wear them.

Homework

Remember that the settings on your phone, laptop, computer, etc., will all be slightly different, and online shops' colours will show other variations. So, it is worth shopping in person so that you can see the colours of a garment and feel the quality of the material too.

Consider which personalities you admire in terms of their dress sense and whether there are elements of their style that you can steal when building your own look.

Whichever celebrity style you steal still must work with your body shape, lifestyle and style personality to ensure you get the most wear out of the items in your wardrobe.

Don't be afraid to mix old and new. Second-hand and vintage pieces from different decades can look fabulous when paired well as an outfit.

Chapter 17

It's Not Just About What You Wear

"I love the feeling of the fresh air on my face and the wind blowing through my hair."

Evel Knievel

As you probably realise, looking good and feeling fantastic is not just about the clothes you wear – it starts from within you and covers way more than just clothing.

What you eat, your lifestyle, the work life you may or may not have and whether you are a social butterfly, or a shy wallflower all have a collective impact.

The phrase "beauty comes from within" is so true and in a world full of choices over what you buy, what you eat, what you do, what you think and who you socialise with or are influenced by affects you more than you may realise until stopping to think about it.

Getting the balance right for you is vital to your physical and mental health. I remember feeling ill as a child. My Mum made me get dressed for a walk around the local graveyard to stop me from feeling sorry for myself and to get some fresh air. To be fair, I did feel a lot better afterwards and was not half as miserable.

Really thinking about the foods you eat and getting a balanced diet that includes fruit and vegetables should not be underrated. The phrase "you are what you eat" is pretty accurate. If you eat lots of fatty processed foods, you won't get all the things your body needs and may find that you put on weight or have outbreaks of spots on your skin as your body tries to shed toxins.

Drinking plenty of water and eating a diet full of the correct nutritional elements, including plenty of fruit and vegetables, helps your body have the right vitamins and minerals needed to function more effectively and will positively impact your skin.

I am not a nutritionist by any means. I understand that some people have food allergies, which may mean they can't eat all the good stuff and may need a dietary supplement to top up those vitamins or minerals that can't be absorbed in other ways.

Following a skincare routine is another key to helping you feel good about yourself. There are many sources of advice from different skincare professionals, both in person and online. Consider investing in a special treat and seek advice in an appointment at your local spa or with a consultant at a beauty counter in a department store. They have received training on the products they sell and can help you build a routine with the right products that work for your skin type.

I went for a consultation at Trinny London this year which was fantastic. I got to try a whole routine of products that suit my skin type and highly recommend their service.

As with your skincare routine, consider the type of makeup you wear or don't wear. Gone are the days of the thick caked-on style. Many forms of base foundation makeup incorporate serums, moisturisers and SPF. Similarly, the range of lip colours and eye makeup is an ever-evolving mixture of colours and chemistry incorporating elements that help protect and moisturise, amongst many other things. You may have a particular brand you like or want to keep your mind open to trying something new; either way, it is worth contacting a representative for the brand to ask for a makeup refresh session. Often, there is a charge that can be offset against any purchase that you make. Go in with an open mind and try what the brand's representative suggests – you may be pleasantly surprised. They usually have many valuable application tips you can pick up, too.

Exercise, in some form or another, plays a huge part in looking and feeling good. When you are active, your body releases "happy" chemicals that help you to feel good and refreshed. Exercise doesn't have to mean going to the gym; it could be walking around the block or having a boogie in the kitchen whilst listening to your favourite track on the radio.

If you have pets, it could be taking the dog for a walk or pushing a shopping trolley around your local supermarket and then packing and lifting your bags into the car. It's all movement and exercise and it all helps. If you are feeling tired or stressed or your mind is blank, then getting moving – especially outdoors in fresh air can be a total game-changer rather than sitting in a chair or at a desk.

Don't forget that exercise is not just for your body but also applies to your brain. Keeping your brain active by reading a book and doing puzzles or crosswords helps keep it ticking. Exercising your brain in the form of mindfulness time is also crucial especially if you live a busy lifestyle. It may be that your mindfulness comes from meditation. I've always found this challenging and never know if I'm doing it right. Still, the ability to zone out of the present to somewhere else may happen when you exercise or shower. When swimming, running or doing something repetitively on autopilot, your mind may wander away from what you are actually doing to think about other things instead. This may be where all your great ideas and creativity come from.

Whatever your form of mindfulness, just having that downtime to drift away from the pressures of day-to-day life is valuable in helping you cope with whatever challenges life throws your way, especially when they are unexpected.

Having a challenge or a goal for something you are working towards can keep you focused or even just a habit you do each day. This may be a virtual challenge – I walked Lands End to John O'Groats virtually during lockdown on that one hour of exercise we were allowed daily. Your habit may be walking up and down the stairs three times after lunch so you don't get that sleepy post-lunch feeling, or maybe you have three things on a to-do list for the day and when they are done, you have a sense of achievement that spurs you on to do other things.

The people you surround yourself with play a part in your mental health. We all enjoy the time we spend with our friends. When connecting with like-minded people with similar interests who you can laugh with or share your challenges with, you can support one another, too. Surround yourself with the people who ooze positive vibes rather than negativity. Be the person who organises a group of friends you may not have seen in a while to get together. Everyone will reconnect where you last left off, keeping those friendships and support networks going.

All these elements are like the pieces of a jigsaw that come together to build up the picture of who you are and help you feel good about yourself, which will give you confidence in how you show up each day.

You may want to share your Look Good and Feel Fantastic journey with friends – or you may want to keep quiet and wait for them to notice and compliment you.

Homework

Consider the type of foods you eat and how to incorporate a balance in your diet.

Drink plenty of water – cut the caffeine a bit...and a bit less alcohol to notice how this makes you feel and how it impacts your skin.

Create a skincare routine and follow it – don't go to bed with your makeup on at night no matter how tired you feel.

Consider seeking advice and trying out a skincare or makeup refresh – it may give you some new techniques or colours you may not have previously considered.

Get moving – exercise doesn't have to be a formal gym session. Consider how you can get moving in a way that suits the demands of your lifestyle.

Create time for mindfulness. A little quiet time to relax or something that enables you to zone out and give your brain a break.

Surround yourself with positive people – keep up those friendships or contact someone you haven't seen for a long time. They will probably be thrilled to hear from you!

LOOK GOOD AND FEEL FANTASTIC

Chapter 18

Colour Psychology; The Science Bit

"Monday morning blues?
Why not change the colour of your Monday to yellow
and brighten up the coming week?"
Kanika Saxena

Colour psychology studies how different colours can impact your emotions and behaviour. There is no exact science as it is all open to interpretation and can vary depending on which part of the world you are in. There may be variations by country in local customs and traditions, too.

Fashion designers use colour psychology to influence trends. Each year, there is a Pantone Colour of the Year, used as the base palette that reflects the cultural mood of the moment.

In addition to finding the right colour shades for your clothes that work for your skin tone, hair colouring and style personality, it is worth considering the impact of how you feel when you wear specific colours. Some shades may instantly be mood-uplifting for you, whereas others may make you feel drained and lacking in energy.

Whilst scientific, the impact that colours convey can still vary from person to person depending on their own experiences and interpretations. For example, you may see red as a colour of passion, whereas someone else may find it intimidating, like the saying "a red rag to a bull".

Using colour in clothing helps you communicate how you feel and may or may not want to interact with other people. You may already be doing this without really thinking about it. Everywhere in day-to-day life, there are general associations with colours, for example, black being the colour of mourning, white dresses at weddings, lighter shades of clothing in summer that reflect the light to keep us cool and darker shades of clothing in winter that absorb the light and keep us warmer.

A lot of science is involved that we don't usually stop to think about, such as the impact of colour on the brain. You may have memories attached to specific colours or feel that a colour positively impacts you but has the opposite effect on someone else.

Colour interpretations can vary, but you may already understand what different colours portray. Many companies carefully consider the colours they use in their branding or adverts. The colour of your outfit is something to think carefully about if you decide to be photographed in a work context.

Red symbolises anger, love, passion, power and confidence – all strong emotions. It's a colour that triggers our fight or flight response to danger, so is a colour to wear when you want to feel confident or stand out. It's great to wear in small doses for online meetings, so it's not overpowering.

Orange symbolises enthusiasm, attention, happiness, fun and energy. Again, it's a colour that says "look at me!!" but is not as confrontational as red. Wear orange when you want to feel confident – It's an excellent choice if you are presenting as it's a colour that people often see as creative, fun and sociable, so is helpful when you want to hold people's attention.

Yellow says warmth, attention, optimism, energy and happiness – the colour of sunshine and all those feel-good factors that come from soaking up vitamin D on a sunny day. Wear yellow when you want to feel happy or to uplift your mood. Again, it can help you stand out on social media, but it may be too much if you work in a formal office environment.

Green is associated with luck, envy, safety, healing and nature. It can symbolise a sense of calm, reassuring and approachability. Wear green when you want to feel grounded or refreshed. It's a great colour to wear for important meetings or when expecting to meet new people at networking or social events where you may not know the other guests, especially if you find these occasions stressful.

Blue is the colour of stability, productivity, loyalty, competence, wisdom, tranquillity, trust and calmness. When you think about it, the sky and the sea are blue and join together when you look at the horizon. They are dependable for always being there which promotes a sense of calm. Looking at a blue sea can slow your heart rate, deepen your breathing and calm you down if you are stressed or anxious. Wear blue when you want to feel confident and to diffuse a stressful situation. It's an excellent colour for a job interview to promote professionalism and encourage trust.

Purple is associated with gowns of royalty, wealth, mystery, luxury and imagination (or, in my case, a particular brand of chocolate.) Wear purple when you want to feel special and to stand out. It's another excellent choice to wear for online meetings or when you want to feel a bit mysterious.

Soft pink is the colour of romance, kindness, calmness, nurturing and compassion, so it's an excellent choice for special family occasions. However, a hot, bright fuchsia pink is suitable for when you want to feel bold or in control.

Brown is the colour associated with nature, warmth, reliability, security and strength. Wear brown when you need to step back, relax, and want to blend in rather than stand out but do wear it sparingly to avoid looking boring or too masculine.

Black is the colour of mystery, power, professionalism, confidence and elegance, which is why the LBD (Little Black Dress) is a popular iconic wardrobe staple. However, it is also generally seen as the colour of mourning and sorrow, so it is not the colour to wear if you are feeling low. Wear black when you want to feel strong; it's a colour to be taken seriously and will help you be seen as someone in authority.

White is the colour of peace, cleanliness and innocence. Wear white to feel uplifted and fresh. It's an excellent option for a new start i.e. that blank piece of paper effect.

Grey is a neutral shade and balanced. However, it can give the impression of lifelessness, feeling low or lacking energy. It's a good idea to pair grey with another colour to offset this effect.

All colours have their shades within them, so the paler tones of the colours will dissolve the impression that the colour gives. In contrast, stronger tones of the colours will enhance the impression that the colour provides, which is worth thinking about when considering how colours can influence your mood and that of others.

Homework

Consider the impact of how you feel when you wear specific colours.

Consider if there are times when you may want to harness the power of colour psychology in what you are doing inside or outside of work.

Chapter 19

You Wear It Well

"You can be gorgeous at thirty, charming at forty and irresistible for the rest of your life!"

Coco Chanel

Looking good and feeling fantastic is all about your choices along the way.

Choosing a healthy, active lifestyle and eating a balanced diet are the foundations for the inner you, along with recognising and acting on your mental health needs.

Choosing clothes that fit your body shape, in colours that suit you and with detailing in all the right places will really help you, provided you have your foundations right in the first place by wearing the right underwear and especially the right bra size. Hence, if you only take one thing away from this book, please get a professional bra fitting at an independent shop/qualified bra fitter. I promise you that this alone will be an absolute game-changer for you.

When you feel good and look good, it can do wonders for your self-confidence! Feeling good inside also has to be feeling good on the outside and being comfortable in what you wear. Soft, comfortable clothing that isn't itchy or annoying that you enjoy wearing and feels like a second skin to you, will also promote feeling good in your inner self.

When you feel good, you stand slightly taller and stand out. You will find that your body language changes. Rather than hunching over trying to hide or blend in, your posture changes to be more upright, shoulders back, head held high and ready to take on the world.

Once you have identified your style inspirations and worked out your own style personality, this helps you find the pieces that work for you, saving you time and money in the long run. The aim of the game is to choose well so that you buy less and then look after it to make it last.

Knowing the terminology we discussed in Chapter 6 will help you when online shopping for clothes. You can scan the details in the descriptions and understand whether the garment may work for you before ordering, saving you the hassle of returning items that are clearly wrong.

Listen to your gut! When you put something on or hold it next to you and look in the mirror pay attention to your gut feeling. It might be a definite yes, no or a "hmm – not sure". If it's the latter there is a good chance that the item will sit in your wardrobe as it's not quite right for you – if it's a style or colour that you are not used to wearing I would suggest you sleep on it before buying and see how you feel about it first.

Have fun with your clothes whilst still dressing for your occasion and lifestyle. Making sure you can find three ways of wearing each piece in your wardrobe will mean you can slowly build a capsule wardrobe with longevity. This may allow you to invest in a more expensive/quality garment as you will not need to buy clothes as often, saving you money in the longer term. You can still follow colour and design trends via accessories or introduce just a few pieces to your capsule each season.

Consider rethinking your skincare and make-up routines. Make-up, in particular, makes a difference to your overall look. If you feel that your make-up look is a little dated and you are unsure where to go next, book an appointment for a refresher and keep an open mind. As a teenager in the 1980s, I used to wear pink, yellow and blue eyeshadow in stripes all at the same time, which would look ridiculous today!

Another option is to book a photo shoot with a professional makeup artist. Your local photography studios often offer this as a package, making it a great gift. The professional make-up artist can give you advice and if you are someone who finds it hard to look at yourself in a mirror, then looking at yourself in a photograph can give you a different perspective as well as working as your style guide and confidence booster for days when you may be feeling a little low.

If you buy your clothes from popular online or high street retailers, inevitably, at some point, you will bump into someone else wearing the same garment! Remember, the same garment worn by five different women will look slightly different on every single person depending on their body shape, age, height, style personality, make-up, hair and how they have styled or are wearing the outfit, so if you come across someone else at an event in the same outfit don't panic!

A longer sleeve length can be pushed up for a different look, a skirt with an elasticated waist can be folded over to make it a shorter length or worn over the hips to make it a longer length, or you can remove the attached belt from an item and wear with your own belt instead or go beltless altogether if that style works for you. Alternatively, you may be delighted with how you are wearing your outfit and decide to stick with your look instead and take it as a compliment that you and someone else have chosen the same piece, so obviously, you have good taste!

Sometimes, there are garment breakdowns or wardrobe malfunctions. This is irrespective of how much the garment cost. Accidents can happen or sometimes there is more wear and tear on a favourite item without you noticing. Keeping an elasticated hairband and a couple of safety pins in your purse can help you tweak your outfit should you want or need to, if an unexpected situation occurs. I recently went to an evening event where I drove in my flat shoes taking strappy heels to change into to wear with my maxi dress when I arrived. Unfortunately, as I put my heels on, I discovered that the heel strap for one was missing and must have fallen out on my way from the house to the car in the dark. Thankfully, an elastic band saved the day, which I attached to the shoe and slipped my foot through. Nobody saw the elastic band attaching the shoe to my ankle beneath my dress. Amazingly, it held the shoe in place all night, so the problem was solved.

Homework

Consider the big picture in how your clothes make you feel – physically and mentally. If you are unsure about a garment, you will probably not wear it, so "sleep on it" and revisit it before you make the purchase.

If you haven't already, get a professional bra fitting – it will be a game-changer!

Consider a makeup and/or skincare refresh appointment to pick up some alternative colours or learn more about applying your makeup from a professional makeup artist.

Keep an elastic hairband and a couple of safety pins in your purse for emergency "wardrobe malfunctions."

Conclusion

So there we are! As the satnav would say, "You have reached your destination!"

There is a wealth of information online - Google is a wonderful thing for finding answers to any other questions you may have and viewing images of sleeve types, more pockets or styles of jeans, as there are plenty more than I have covered in this book.

Most style books are pretty cumbersome and have beautiful images inside but are more of a "coffee table book," as I would call them. The intention with this book is to take it with you when you are on the go – read it on the train and keep it handy in a bag as your "go to" style guide.

Thank you for taking me on this journey with you. I hope you have enjoyed this book and found helpful tips so that you buy less by choosing well. When you look after your clothing it will last for many years to come, helping you to look good and feel fantastic in the process, too.

About the Author

At 15, Angela signed with a model agency for a short spell of catwalk modelling before becoming Carnival Queen of Great Britain at 19.

She moved to London to study alongside a professional career in Human Resources and Employment Law, enjoying some informal modelling before moving to Surrey, where she met her husband, and they started their family.

Angela has worked for a high-street fashion retailer before working in the UK for a French Fashion Brand as a Style Consultant alongside promotions and outdoor events work with Pirate FM Radio Station.

She now works as a Style Consultant with Tortue.UK, helping women look good and feel fantastic! She likes to keep fit, enjoying the outdoors by swimming, dog walks and a little running, completing the London, Paris and New York Marathons over three successive years.

Angela likes laughing, good food, cooking and creative projects plus volunteering for British Divers Marine Life Rescue at beach rescues for sick/injured seals and dolphins, helping to care for ill/wounded seals at the BDMLR Cornwall Seal Hospital and completing charity challenges to fundraise for causes that are important to her.

About PublishU

PublishU enables you to tell your story or communicate your message by writing and publishing a book worldwide.

"I never thought I would be able to write a book, let alone in 100 days... now I'm asking what else have I told myself that I can't do that I actually can?'"

PublishU Author

To find out more visit

www.PublishU.com

LOOK GOOD AND FEEL FANTASTIC

Printed in Great Britain
by Amazon

62883351R00100